Inspirational Native American Stories for Kids

Empowering Tales of Tradition, Wisdom and Resilience — Inspiring Cultural Pride, Empathy and Hope

Welcome Aboard, Check Out This Limited-Time Free Bonus!

Ahoy, reader! Welcome to the Ahoy Publications family, and thanks for snagging a copy of this book! Since you've chosen to join us on this journey, we'd like to offer you something special.

Check out the link below for a FREE e-book filled with delightful facts about American History.

But that's not all - you'll also have access to our exclusive email list with even more free e-books and insider knowledge. Well, what are ye waiting for? Click the link below to join and set sail toward exciting adventures in American History.

Access your bonus here
https://ahoypublications.com/
Or, Scan the QR code!

Table of Contents

Part 1: Inspiring Native American Stories for Kids

Captivating Tales of Tradition, Wisdom, and Resilience to Nurture Cultural Appreciation and Empathy

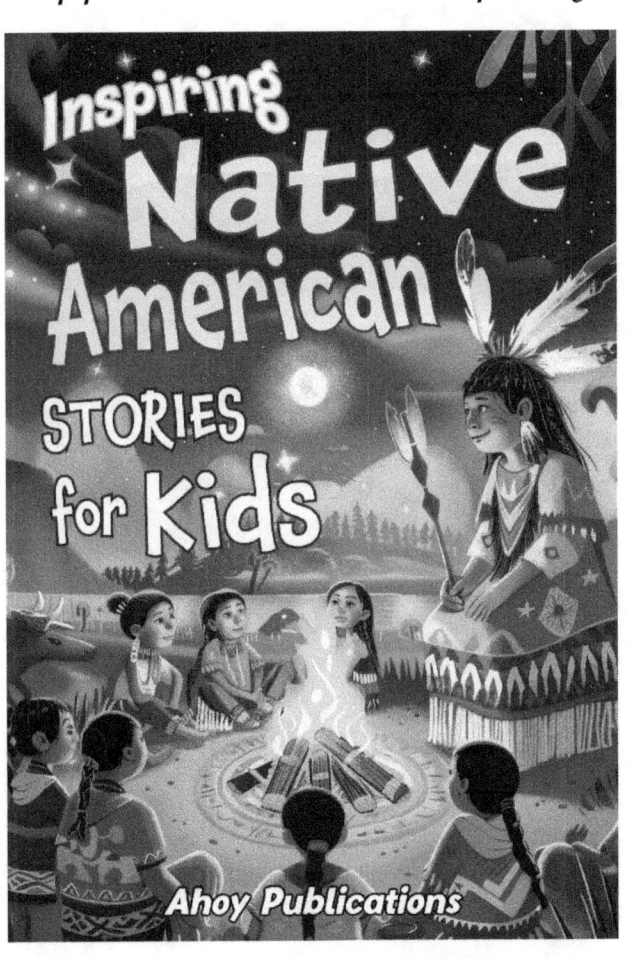

Introduction

Ever since the first people gathered around fires, storytelling has been a way to share the highs and lows of life with family and friends. Long ago, people learned important lessons when life was tough with wild hunts and deep connections to nature. They turned these lessons into amazing myths and stories about big beasts, powerful gods, and mysterious spirits. These stories have been passed down from parents to kids for thousands of years; now, you can read them, too!

The Native Americans have always felt a special bond with the earth, the air, and the bright sun. Their unique way of seeing the world comes from their smart ways, strong hearts, and old traditions. These stories are filled with adventures and lessons from the past that still matter today. As you read, you'll feel like you're part of the action, meeting brave heroes and magical creatures along the way.

Imagine reading these stories by a campfire, the air filled with the smell of s'mores and the sounds of crickets and rustling trees—it's the perfect setting for tales that are exciting and a bit spooky. Or read them at bedtime and let your dreams be adventures. These stories will stick with you forever, teaching you about the magic of nature, the strength of sticking together, the bravery of heroes, and the hope for a better future.

As you dive into this book, you'll connect with the wisdom of many different Native American tribes. Picture yourself in their thrilling tales of adventure and bravery, meeting wise chiefs, magical animals, and fearless warriors. Discover secrets and wonders that time almost forgot. These ancient American traditions are just waiting for you to explore. Get ready for a thrilling journey into history with each page you turn!

Chapter 1: Stories of the Ancestors: Timeless Legends

What Is Native American Folklore?

Folklore is the stories and customs passed down from generation to generation. [1]

Folklore is the stories and customs that get passed down from generation to generation. Some stories are so old that it is difficult to tell where they came from. They sit so deep in the souls of people that it is impossible to separate these stories from a culture. What makes people different from all the animals on earth is their ability to tell stories and pass them on to their children. Folklore is created when many people keep passing on a tradition so much that it becomes a part of who they are. These stories get built upon over time because the lessons they teach are important for new generations. Folklore can be art, verbal traditions, music, or religion, but they all hold important messages for those who receive them.

These stories highlight the Native American bond with nature. '

The following tales include the creation story of the Hopi, the legend of Tigguk from the Inuit tribes, and the Wampanoag tale of Maushop the Giant. These stories highlight the Native American bond with nature so that you get a better understanding of how everything is connected and your responsibility to care for the plants and animals around you.

Through mystical tales of creation and adventure, you get the opportunity to travel the same road that the generations of children traveled before you. Elders of these tribes have repeated these fables for hundreds of years, and now they have reached you so that your imagination can run wild, too.

Creation Myths of Different Tribes

Hopi Tribe Creation Story

Nature is extremely important for indigenous American culture. They understand that without the natural world, people will die, so they honor it. The respect for nature that Indigenous people have is sown into their creation myths. Indigenous people do not see humans as more important than the natural world but rather look at people as part of a complicated spiderweb that connects everything.

The Hopi people understand that the Earth does not belong to humanity; people belong to the Earth. She is the mother of humankind. The Hopi tribe forms part of a larger group called the Pueblo, who come from parts of modern Arizona and New Mexico. The Hopi story of creation is one of the most interesting creation stories in the world.

At the beginning of time, before anything else existed, there were two great beings whose power had no limits. One of these beings was the Spider Woman. She has even more powers than the web-slinger, who wears red and blue tights. The Spider Woman is the Goddess of Earth and is the caregiver of all people on the globe. The other mighty being who was there at the beginning of time is Tawa, the Sun God, who controls everything in the vast sky you look up to at night. He moves the planets, lights up the stars, and throws the meteors that whizz super-fast through the air.

Tawa and the Spider Woman were lonely after spending millions and millions of years together. They had the bright idea to create more living things so they would no longer have to be alone. Tawa ruled the upper worlds, and Spider-Woman ruled the lower worlds. The Land of Shimmering Waters is between the two worlds, where they created the lovely Earth you call home.

Tawa, the Sun God, and the Spider Woman begin a beautiful dance. They twirl around, leaping through all the worlds and swaying and singing at the top of their lungs, creating a powerful, magical wind that fills every corner of the universe. From this magical wind, all the flowers on Earth spring up. They are very colorful and bright. Every color of the rainbow can be seen in their gorgeous petals, and their green leaves and stems stretch into the sky with gratitude to their creators.

After their song and dance session, Tawa feels tired, so he lays down, looking at all the beautiful flowers they just created. He starts to daydream about all kinds of birds flying through the sky, soaring around the mountaintops, and zipping in between the forest trees. He imagines big and small fish jumping through the rivers and diving in and out of the ocean. He thinks of all the trees, some so small that they scrape your ankles and others so giant that they touch the clouds. He dreams of all the animals on Earth, from the mighty Bison running on the open plains to the rattlesnake that wiggles its warning shaker and even the tiny ants who pinch your back when you lay in the tall grass.

The Spider Woman sees Tawa's daydream, and it impresses her. She is amazed at all the different wonderful creatures that Tawa imagines. She is so impressed that hiding all these incredible beings in a dream is not enough for her. The Spider Woman decides to create all of Tawa's dreams from the clay on the Earth, molding them carefully with her loving hands. To this day, the Hopi people honor Tawa and the Spider Woman, who look after them and give them everything they need from the natural world they created. They are like a cosmic mother and father looking after all the people on the planet.

Legendary Heroes: Create Your Own Legend

The Story of Tiggak

Native Americans (or indigenous people) do not all come from one tribe. They have thousands of different traditions, languages, and stories. The Inuit tribes come from the cold parts of America, like Canada and Alaska, where the icy winds bite your skin. Rubbing their hands around a blazing campfire, wrapped in thick furs as the wind whistles through the night, the Elders tell the story of the brave Tiggak.

Long ago, in ancient times, there was a brave and humble man named Tiggak. Food was running low in his village, but because a vicious storm was approaching, many of the hunters were afraid to venture out. As their desperation grew, Tiggak and his son took on the impossible task of going into the rough seas to fish. The strong winds and snow formed ice crystals on their hair while their fingers went numb from tightly clutching their spears.

They got into their skin-covered boat, known as a umiak. The waters grew rougher as waves the size of skyscrapers bashed their small umiak up, down, left, and right. Unfortunately, Tiggak's beloved son passed away in the chaos, so he was forced to carry his body back to the shore. As his eyes welled up with tears and his heart shattered into a hundred pieces, Tiggak buried his son and piled stones on top of his grave.

The skin-covered boat is called an Umiak.[8]

Tiggak could not stand to be separated from his son, so he never returned to the village, choosing instead to construct a home next to where he buried his son. As his grief finally put him to sleep, Tiggak heard rustling outside of his igloo. He woke up, grabbing his spear and carefully approaching the potential danger. He found a fox, a hare, a walrus, and an ice bear digging up his son's grave.

In a heated rage, Tiggak yelled out and, with his mighty strength, attacked the animals, disturbing his son's grave. They tried to fight back but were no match for his incredible power. As he pinned the animals down with his spear, they begged him to spare their lives, explaining why they were doing what they did.

The fox pleaded with Tiggak, saying, "I'm only doing this because I need to get my teeth." The walrus explained, "The only way I can get my whiskers is from your son." The hare explained, "All the internal organs that keep me alive I will get from your son." The ice bear completed their explanation by telling Tiggak, "The only way we can stay alive is by stealing from the dead." Tiggak calmed down because he finally understood that the animals did not take these actions out of cruelty but because they needed to. They taught Tiggak a lesson about the balance of nature and the cycles of life and death. Tiggak let them go, and they repaid his kindness by making sure that his village never went hungry again by always providing them with bountiful hunts.

Maushop the Giant

The Wampanoag people live on the southeastern coast of Massachusetts. Their name in English means "The First People of the Light." Much like many other Native American cultures, the Wampanoag people had a strong connection to the natural world and their surroundings because it was so deeply tied to their daily lives. The Wampanoag people understood that everything is connected. Humanity is part of a complicated and sensitive system, so you must respect nature. The Wampanoag people understood that they could not only selfishly take from nature, but they had to give back because they are part of the Circle of Life and have a duty to look after the plants, animals, rivers, and seas. The story of Maushop the Giant explains how the Wampanoag people learned about their role in the natural cycles of the world.

One day, long ago, the Wampanoag people came across a strong and friendly giant named Maushop, who lived alongside many other magical beings. One of the magical creatures who was Maushop's best friend was a giant frog that could leap as high as the tallest mountain. Maushop was so powerful, and his muscles were so big that when he moved his arms, his clothes would often burst around his bulging biceps. The Wampanoag people loved Maushop because although he was so big and strong, he was gentle and would never harm anybody.

Maushop lived a life of excitement and adventure. He would swim in Popponesset Bay on hot summer days, swinging his windmill arm as he splashed in the cold water. At night, he would make humungous fires on the beach that could be seen from 1,000 miles away! Maushop used these fires to cook whales and other sea creatures because his huge body gave him a massive appetite. Maushop's amazing life made the Wampanoag people love him even more, so they became great friends.

Maushop began helping the Wampanoag with their daily chores. '

Maushop began helping the Wampanoag with their daily chores. When they needed fire, he would carry large bundles of heavy wood on his back, and when they were hungry, he would dive deep into the ocean to herd whales onto the shore for them. Maushop started doing so much for the people that they became lazy, just sitting around all day relaxing and doing nothing.

Kehtean the Great Spirit saw this and was unhappy with how the humans had started behaving. The Great Spirit knew that everyone needed to do their part for the Circle of Life to be strong and unbreakable. With a bellowing voice, he called out to Maushop, who got up and ran to him immediately. Kehtean explained that although

Maushop loved the people, he needed to stop doing everything for them because their laziness was going to cause trouble for all living beings in the Circle of Life. When one part of the Circle is out of balance, it can cause everything to collapse, which will lead to catastrophe throughout the land.

Maushop understood what the Great Spirit said, so he decided to leave the people he loved so much. He dove into the ocean, waving goodbye to the Wampanoag and the magical friends he was leaving behind as he went on to greater adventures. When he got far into the ocean, almost out of sight to everybody standing on the sandy shore, the Great Spirit turned him into a giant white whale to spend his days exploring the vast ocean.

Maushop dove into the ocean and spent many days exploring it.[5]

Maushop's best friend, the giant frog, would miss his buddy with whom he spent so much time going on all sorts of adventures. He wailed with sorrow, shaking with sadness as he saw his friend swim out into the distance. Kehtean felt sorry for the giant frog who was crying endless tears. He transformed the frog into a huge stone set on top of Gay Head Cliff. Whenever the Womaponoag people look at this stone, they are reminded of how much the Great Spirit cares for them.

The Wampanoag people learned how to get their chores done.[6]

Now that Maushop was gone, the Wampanoag people began scratching their heads, unsure of what to do next because the giant had been doing everything for them for so long. Eventually, they began working together and figuring it out. They learned to work with the water, sea creatures, plants, and animals to meet all of their needs. This is how the Wampanoag people got back in line with the Circle of Life, taking their place as the ones who care for nature and honoring it with their prayers, rituals, and respectful activities.

Create Your Own Legend

1. What lessons have you learned from the legends of Tiggak, Maushop the Giant, Tawa, and the Spider Woman?

_____

_____

_____

_____

_____

_____

2. Which outdoor location in nature is your favorite? Is it the park, the beach, the forest, or somewhere else?

_____

_____

_____

_____

_____

_____

3. Write a story about a legend that you create. Set the story in your favorite place where you spend time in nature.

_____

_____

_____

_____

_____

4. Use a notebook or a piece of paper to draw your legend going on an adventure.

5. Remember that the adventure should teach people an important lesson you want them to learn – like bravery, patience, kindness, love, or caring for nature.

Chapter 2: Native Courage and Leadership

Native American history is riddled with stories woven by the threads of courage, sacrifice, and triumph. It's common knowledge how the Indigenous Americans suffered at the hands of the settlers who hailed from other lands; however, this fact does not take away from the victories they secured in an attempt to protect their land and heritage. Their tales are full to the brim with leaders who defied the odds and faced off against an enemy that surpassed them in weaponry and tactical warfare to preserve their culture.

Their tales are full to the brim with leaders who defied the odds and faced off against an enemy.[7]

In this chapter, you'll find yourself encapsulated with the tales of two of the most famous leaders known in the history of the American Natives: leaders who carved their impact in the young minds of the generations that followed them.

Chief Sitting Bull, the Renowned Leader of the Hunkpapa Lakota Sioux

Sitting Bull. The spiritual and military leader of the Sioux warriors. '

The spiritual and military leader of the Sioux warriors is well known for his infamous victory against General George Armstrong Custer at the Battle of Little Bighorn. His fame traveled even further after being involved in the popular Wild West Show with Bill Cody. However, there is more to his story than being a victorious leader and a so-so celebrity. So, who is Sitting Bull?

Life and Background

The Hunkpapa Lakota leader was born in 1831 in the land now commonly known as South Dakota, near the Grand River. When he was born, his father, the chief, named him "Jumping Badger." At a young age, he seemed slightly challenged when it came to his fighting skills and didn't show much promise when it came to waging wars. He was, therefore, called "Slow" -a temporary name for his calm and deliberate attitude until he could prove himself worthy of a better name.

It didn't take long before the young warrior managed to shake off the title given to him earlier. At the young age of 10, he managed to kill his first buffalo, and when he was only 14 years old, he was involved in a fight with rival Crow Indians. During the fight, *Slow* managed to hit one of the enemy warriors with a coup stick, a maneuver called the "count coup." As a result, he was awarded an eagle feather that he wore proudly on his head and was renamed "Tantanka Yotanka," which translates to Sitting Bull or Buffalo Bull who sits down.

At that time, the young man had already proved he possessed all four Lakota virtues: wisdom, bravery, generosity, and fortitude.

Afterward, he joined the Silent Eaters, the Kit Fox Warrior Society, and Strong Heart societies, all of which have the tribe's wellbeing as their main priority. He assisted in expanding the Sioux's hunting grounds into the western territories previously owned and inhabited by the Crow, Shoshone, Assiniboine, and others.

Sitting Bull served as the leader of the entire Lakota Sioux nation, a position never held by any before him, and he was quite vocal with his opinions to avoid all manners of engagement with the white man when others seemed eager to do otherwise. He famously stated, "I have seen nothing that the white man has... which is as good as our right to roam and live on the open plains as we choose."

The fierce leader earned spiritual prominence during his time as the leader of the Lakotas. He often received visions from Wakan-Tanka, "the Everywhere Spirit," where many followers claimed they *DID* come true. Not long after, he officially added "spiritual leader" to the many other titles he had earned.

The Battle of Little Bighorn

The Battle of Little Bighorn.[9]

Sitting Bull was no stranger to skirmishes with the U.S. government. In June of 1863, he faced off against the U.S. Army after federal agents withheld food from the Sioux that resided in the reservations as payback for the Minnesota Uprising.

He fought them again in July of 1864 when General Alfred Sully laid siege and surrounded one of the Indian trading villages in the battle of Killdeer Mountain.

These confrontations did nothing but cement Sitting Bull's resolve to not sign any peace treaties with the white man who aimed to eventually relocate his people to a reservation.

These ideals were not unanimous among all Indian leaders, though. In 1868, Red Cloud, chief of the Oglala Teton Dakota Sioux, along with 24 other leaders, went on to sign the Fort Laramie Treaty with Lieutenant General William Tecumseh Sherman. The agreement declared the foundation of the Great Sioux Reservation, along with granting them additional land in Nebraska, Wyoming, and South Dakota.

Sitting Bull's dislike for the treaty earned him much favor among his followers, providing him with more allies (friends) from the Cheyenne and Arapaho tribes.

It didn't take long before he was proven right in his convictions. In 1874, gold was discovered in a sacred site of the Sioux in the Black Hills, which lay within the borders agreed upon for the newly-founded reservation. Needless to say, all peace agreements went out the window once the white man caught wind of the news of the unearthed fortunes.

Many white settlers started falsely claiming the land as their own, while the U.S. government didn't shy away from supporting their illegal claims. They declared new borders in June of 1876 and started threatening the Sioux, who refused to leave.

Among those expected to relocate were members of Sitting Bull's village, who were asked to leave their homes and travel 240 miles in the unforgiving cold.

Holding his stance and refusing to move from his ancestral land, Sitting Bull started preparations for a showdown with the U.S. government. In June 1876, he scored a victory against General George Crook with a group that included Arapaho, Sioux, and Cheyenne. He then moved his army to the Valley of Little Bighorn, where his infamous battle took place.

While camping in Little Bighorn, Sitting Bull took part in the Ceremonial Sun Dance, where he reportedly danced for 36 hours straight and made 50 sacrificial cuts on his arms right before descending into a spiritual trance. During his trance, he observed a vision where he saw U.S. soldiers descending from the sky like grasshoppers. He believed this was a sign of an upcoming victory over their oppressors.

He was not wrong. On the 25th of June, General George Custer led around 300 men (the numbers vary from one account to another) into the Valley, where he was met with 3,000 strong native men on the battlefield. Sitting Bull, being older than the normal fighting age, ensured the safety of the women and children while handing over the army's leadership to Crazy Horse. His two nephews, White Bull and One Bull, took part in the battle, protected by their uncle's medicine. The Sioux men fought bravely, taking out the entire force of General Custer's army in a swift victory, later known as *Custer's Last Stand.*

The Aftermath

As a result of the victory, the U.S. government felt scorned and humiliated that they doubled down on their pursuits of the Sioux men. The white settlers started targeting the livelihood of the Sioux by killing the buffalo herds they depended on to survive.

In return, Sitting Bull wisely decided to protect his flock by leading them to Canada in May of 1877. However, with little food to go around, the chief was forced to make a deal with the U.S. Army, where he surrendered himself in exchange for the absolution of his people. As a result of his sacrifice, he was taken prisoner at South Dakota's Fort Randall for two years, and then he was sent to the Standing Rock Reservation.

Wilma Mankiller: The First Female Principal Chief of the Cherokee Nation

Wilma Mankiller is famous for being the first indigenous female chief of the Cherokee nation. [10]

Wilma Mankiller is a modern-day inspiration and hero to a lot of youth in the current century, both of native descent and otherwise. Wilma is famous for being the first indigenous female chief of the Cherokee nation. She was the first woman to be elected to ascend the position of chief in one of the prime native tribes. She may seem familiar if you're used to carrying change in your pocket; she was honored alongside other female pioneers by appearing on a series of quarters!. She spent the better part of her life fighting for the rights of Indigenous Americans.

Early Life

Mankiller was born in Tahlequah, Oklahoma, the nation's capital, on November 18, 1945. She had ten siblings who shared the same name, which translated in Cherokee culture to something akin to Captain or Major. The name referenced the position of a person who watched over the Cherokee population and their villages.

Growing up, Wilma lived in a simple household with no electricity, plumbing, or any means of communication, such as a telephone.

Wilma was moved with her family, ages 10 and 11, as part of the Bureau of Indian Affairs' relocation strategy to a low-income San Francisco neighborhood. She often described this move as her very own little trail of tears about the relocation of her Cherokee ancestors from Tennessee over the Trail of Tears in the 1830s.

The government passed several laws, including the one relocating the aboriginal tribes, intending to sell their reservation lands and break up their settlements. The bills were passed under the pretense of luring the natives to the bigger cities with the promise of better opportunities and jobs when, in fact, it was an effort to assimilate them into the American culture and erase their own.

These bills also resulted in the termination of over 100 tribes and the removal of around 1.3 million acres of native lands. They made sure to shut down health facilities and certain schools in the reservations. Most natives who made the move suffered from poverty and horrible living conditions, finding it extremely hard to get used to life in the city.

Mankiller's Activism

Wilma participated in her first bold act of activism in 1969. She participated in the American Indian Movement's demonstration at Alcatraz, where they claimed a "right of discovery" over the federal prison located in San Francisco Bay. This occupation lasted for 18 months. Reversing the termination measures and reestablishing the cultural institutions and schools on the American Native Island constituted the sum total of the demands.

The American Indian Movement's Flag. "

She made it her mission to instill power and pride back in the Native communities. She became a director at the Native American Youth Center in California, aiming to support and protect the native youth from life on the streets.

Mankiller assisted the indigenous by teaching them about the ins and outs of protecting and exercising treaty rights and tribal sovereignty during the court dispute between Pacific Gas and Electric and the Pit River Tribe. This knowledge traveled back with her when she returned to her Cherokee home.

Mankiller had become a divorced single mother of two girls by 1977, living in her native Oklahoma by a creek in her automobile.

She was eager to work and was successful in landing a position as the economic stimulus coordinator for the Cherokee Nation. This position made her creation of the Cherokee Nation's Community Development Department possible.

Her foundation focused primarily on improving living conditions and supporting the Cherokee nation. Her first project was in Bell, Oklahoma, where 200 native people were living in poverty and without access to water. Empowering the people to work together, and with her ability to organize the workforce and secure enough funding, they succeeded in erecting a 16-mile-long waterline in just 14 months. This feat inspired the movie "The Cherokee Word for Water."

Achievements and Recognition

Wilma became the first female Principal Chief of the Cherokee Nation when she assumed that role in 1985. She served in her role for 10 years, taking care of 140,000 members and being in charge of a budget that amounted to 75 million dollars, which reached 150 million dollars by the end of her time as their leader. During her tenure, tribal enrollment doubled from 68,000 to 170,000. As the tribe chief, she served as the custodian of centuries-long Cherokee traditions and legal codes.

She later established a center for drug misuse prevention and opened three rural healthcare clinics.

She was involved in establishing the U.S. Department of Justice's Office of Tribal Justice. During her leadership, infant mortality significantly declined, while educational accomplishments were on the rise in the Cherokee community.

In 1987, she received the Woman of the Year award from MS Magazine.

She was honored for her efforts to uplift and support her home community by being inducted into the National Women's Hall of Fame in 1993 and by receiving the Presidential Medal of Freedom, the nation's highest civilian honor, from President Bill Clinton in 1998. "Mankiller: A Chief and Her People," her autobiography, was released in 2000.

Wilma Mankiller lost her battle with pancreatic cancer at the age of 64 on April 6th, 2010. She left behind a legacy of strength and resilience for the native youth that came after her.

Test of Knowledge

1. What was Chief Sitting Bull's Birth name, and how did he earn the name Sitting Bull?
2. Who led the charge in the Battle of Little Bighorn?
3. What was the name of the U.S. General that Sitting Bull fought in the battle of Killdeer Mountain?
4. Where was Wilma Mankiller Born?
5. Why was Mankiller's family relocated to San Francisco?
6. When did Mankiller move back to Oklahoma?

Chapter 3: Tales of the Earth and Sky

People have been looking up at the stars for thousands and maybe millions of years. Try to count the stars in the sky. You'll see that it seems like they go on forever. The endless stars in the sky remind humanity how small people are compared to the universe. From the beginning of time, humankind has looked up to the sky to tell stories. The stars, moon, sun, and planets have whispered stories that are kept alive to infinity, and the indigenous people of America have kept many of the tales that the universe has told.

People have been looking up at the stars for thousands and maybe millions of years. [19]

The Great Bear and the Seven Birds

This story is all about the Big Dipper and the constellation that the ancient Romans and Greeks called Corona Borealis. In America, these patterns in the sky are called different names. The Opaskwayak Cree Nation called the Big Dipper "Mista Muskwa," which is the Great Bear. They called the Corona Borealis "Tepahkoop Pinesisuk," or the Seven Birds.

The tale of how the Great Bear and the Seven Birds flew up into the heavens is ancient. Long ago, there were giant bears that roamed the face of the planet. The ground would shake, and dust would fill the air with the force of their huge paws hitting the ground with a thunderous "BOOM!"

The giant bears were so big and strong that every other living thing on earth was terrified of them. The bears used their incredible power to bully everyone to get what they wanted. The leader of these wicked bears was the Great Bear. Whenever he entered a new village, he wanted offerings from the people living there. He went so crazy with power that he eventually stopped asking for offerings, taking whatever his huge arms could carry.

The Great Bear had no love or care in his heart for other living beings. He would ravage a village, crushing anyone who tried to stop him. Sometimes, he ate a village's whole winter supply so they would starve and struggle during the cold months. After years of getting bullied by the Great Bear, a group of elders from several villages came together so that they could figure out how to stop him.

The Great Bear had no love or care in his heart for other living beings. [18]

The village leaders choose from among them seven of the best hunters and trackers. These happened to be the Seven Birds, who were highly skilled at following any beast for thousands of miles. Although the Great Bear was bigger, the Seven Birds were great at working as a team, which is why they were such brilliant hunters.

The Great Bear had his own team of birds who loyally served him for decades. These birds were the Crow, the Raven, and the Magpie. They were scavengers, so they followed the Great Bear around, eating all his leftovers. The Crow, Raven, and Magpie warned the Great Bear of the Seven Birds, who were speeding directly to his den to attack him one morning.

The cowardly bully fled when he heard that the Seven Birds coming for him. They chased him around the Earth four times as his gigantic paws splashed through the salty ocean waves, stumbled through the widest deserts, and climbed over the tallest mountains. In the fourth round, they were moving faster than a rocket, so they zoomed up into the air. The Great Bear's lungs began to burn, and his heart pounded in his chest as he grew more and more tired. Eventually, he got so tired that he turned around to face the skilled hunting birds.

The Robin, or as the Opaskwayak Cree call him, the Pipiciw, who was the bravest of the Seven Birds, dove in beak first, cutting open the Great Bear. The Bear let out a roar and shook with pain, shaking his blood onto all the leaves of the trees, which is why they change color in the fall. A drop of blood fell onto the Robin, which is why all robins today have a red chest.

The Creator of the universe was looking down and watching the chase and fight from the heavens. To honor Robin's bloodline, the Creator gave them speckled eggs that looked like the night sky to remind people of this amazing day when the Great Bear was defeated by tiny birds. He then placed the Seven Birds and the Great Bear in the sky to remind people of all generations of the courage of the Seven Birds. Today, the Great Bear is the Big Dipper constellation, and the Seven Birds are the Corona Borealis constellation.

Today, the Great Bear is the Big Dipper constellation. [14]

The Lost Children

For hundreds of generations, the Black Foot culture has been telling the story of the lost children. This tale is about what happens when people are not kind to the children they have been gifted by the Great Spirit.

A long time ago, close to the beginning of the Earth, six brothers had no parents. The orphan boys did not have a home and would wander from place to place every night, finding a new spot to lay their heads. The cracked lips of their dry mouths stuck together as their stomachs consistently cried out for food. They had no family, so they scavenged the little they had, wearing the ripped clothes that traveling hunters discarded to lighten their loads.

They played and cuddled with the village dogs. The dogs and the boys grew to become great friends and always helped one another in their difficult world. The brothers often shared their beds with the dogs to keep warm on windy nights when the cool breeze ripped through their tattered clothing.

No one in the village treated the children with kindness. The other kids would throw stones at them and chase them with sticks. They made fun of their broken clothing and cackled at their long, matted hair. Once a year, when summer started, the village would open the hunting season by tracking buffalo herds. They would gift the children of the village yellow calf hides to celebrate their success, but they always turned a cold shoulder on the six brothers, giving them nothing.

So tired from how cruelly the village people had treated them all those years, the brothers began

So tired from how cruelly the village people had treated them all those years, the brothers began fantasizing about a better life. [15]

fantasizing about a better life. They were determined to leave the village, and because people had treated them so horribly, they no longer wanted to be human. They began arguing about what they should transform into.

One brother shouted out, "We should be flowers so that we can be beautiful and everyone will admire our gorgeous colors."

The other brothers answered, "If we are flowers, all the buffaloes will eat us."

"Maybe we can be stones. They are strong, and no one can harm them," another brother suggested. "People and animals will trample on us because big rocks break into smaller stones," one of the brothers answered.

"We can be water and flow as far as the land can take us," said one of the brothers. "But then, all the animals and people will drink us," another responded.

Finally, the most intelligent of the boys came up with the perfect solution. They could be stars because they'll be high up in the sky, away from the harsh villagers. Everyone would look at them to tell the change of seasons and admire their beauty. Stars remain forever, so they will always have a place to stay in the sky.

One brother blew on a feather that floated them high up into the sky. He warned everyone to close their eyes and never look back. One of the brothers stubbornly disobeyed and looked down at the village for one last time. He was transformed into the Smoking Star comet.

The boy was transformed into the Smoking Star comet. [16]

The boys floated high into the upper world, landing on a lush green prairie filled with all kinds of aromatic plant life. They approached the huge teepee where Sun Man and his wife, Moon Woman, lived. Sun Man asked the boys why they had traveled so far from Earth. They told him about how unkind the village people were to them. Moon Woman wept with soul-wrenching sadness. She called them the Lost Children.

Sun Man was enraged by the people's hardened hearts. He shone brightly on them, drying up all the water and turning the world into a desert where nothing could grow. All the plants, animals, and people were hungry and thirsty as they breathed in nothing but dust. The dogs that had befriended the boys in the village howled, crying out at Moon Woman and Sun Man to show them mercy.

Sun Man saw the suffering of all the animals and felt sorry for them because he only meant to punish the unkind humans. He sent them rain that brought back all the plants, trees, and rivers for the animals and people to enjoy. The Lost Children are now the Pleiades stars bunched up together in the sky far from the village, reminding people to always be kind to children. They are surrounded by many smaller stars, which are the dogs who found their way back to their lost human friends.

Raven Steals the Light

This story of the cunning trickster, Raven, comes from the Haida people. In the early days of the Earth, there lived a powerful chief who loved his daughter more than anything on the planet. He always got her gifts to show how much he cared for her. One day, the chief took the sun and moon out of the sky and into his large teepee as a gift for his daughter. She leaped with excitement, thanking her beloved father for this incredible present.

Due to the sun and moon now being shielded in the chief's private home, the entire world was pitch black and covered in a blanket of darkness. Nobody could hunt or fish because it was too difficult to see. They either stumbled around, tripping over everything, or crawled on their hands and knees to feel the ground.

The Raven was the most intelligent of all the birds. [17]

The Raven was the most intelligent of all the birds. He said that he would go get the moon and sun back from the chief. The Raven tried to charm the chief with his fancy words, but the stubborn leader would not give him the sun or the moon because it made his daughter so happy. The Raven knew he would need to come up with a plan.

One night, when the chief's daughter went to the river to drink some water, the Raven shape-shifted into a tiny fish and dove into her cup. The daughter never noticed the small fish and swallowed him whole. The Raven began to grow in her belly, transforming into a baby, and the daughter gave birth to a boy named Raven. As Raven grew, he asked his grandfather for the sun and the moon, which the loving chief openly gave to his grandson. Raven returned the sun and the moon to the sky so the people could now once again hunt under the moonlight and sunlight.

Shoot for the Stars Quiz

Write down the letter with the right answer to each question. The answers are at the bottom of the quiz. Do not peak before you complete the quiz. When you are finished, check your answers to see how well you've done.

1. **What is the moral of the story of the Great Bear and the Seven Birds?**
    a. If you work as a team, you can take down big challenges.
    b. A and C.
    c. You should never use your power to bully others.
    d. If you train hard, you will be able to run fast.

2. **What is the Great Bear's Name in the Opaskwayak Cree language?**
    a. Tepahkoop Pinesisuk.
    b. Tigguk.
    c. Flower.
    d. Mista Muskwa.

3. **The Corona Borealis constellation is also known by which name in the Opaskwayak Cree Nation?**
    a. The Big Dipper.
    b. Tepahkoop Pinesisuk.
    c. Mista Muskwa.
    d. The Small Dipper.

4. **Why did the six brothers run away from the village in the story of The Lost Children?**
    a. The village people were unkind to them.
    b. They didn't like the taste of buffalo.
    c. The camp dogs were always biting them.
    d. They wanted to see how fast they could run.

5. **What did the Sun Man do to punish the humans in the story of The Lost Children?**
    a. He flooded the village.
    b. He did nothing.
    c. He caused a drought and dried out the world, so the people were hungry and thirsty.
    d. He made mosquitoes bite the people while they slept.

6. How big was the new home that the Lost Children slept in with Sun Man and Moon Woman, his wife?

    a. The size of the Grand Canyon.

    b. As big as the sky.

    c. Tall like a skyscraper.

    d. As big as a celebrity mansion.

7. Which Indigenous Nation does the story of The Lost Children come from?

    a. Cheyenne.

    b. Apache.

    c. Cherokee.

    d. Black Foot.

8. In the story "Raven Steals the Light," what happened to the people when the chief first put the sun and the moon in his home?

    a. It got so dark nobody could hunt or fish.

    b. Schoolchildren could not study.

    c. It got cold outside.

    d. Everyone was afraid of the dark.

9. What skill did the Raven use to get back the sun and moon?

    a. Strength and bravery.

    b. Intelligence and cunning.

    c. Love and care.

    d. Beauty.

10. Which indigenous nation does the story of "Raven Steals the Light" come from?

    a. The Haida.

    b. Black Foot.

    c. The Pueblo.

    d. The Aztecs.

Chapter 4: Spirit of the Buffalo: Stories of Community

The Native Americans always knew how important it was to respect other living beings. Their stories speak about how, in nature, everyone and everything is connected and depends on each other. This chapter brings you two tales about the creature the Native Americans have a powerful connection to — the buffalo.

Their stories speak about how, in nature, everyone and everything is connected and depends on each other. [18]

The first story is about a beautiful young woman sent as a messenger to teach the Lakota how to live peacefully and happily together. The second tale shows how the Plains tribes explain the origin of the buffalo hunt — the activity that helped them survive and build strong communities.

The Lakota Legend of the White Buffalo Calf Woman

A few American Indian tribes considered the buffalo a priceless gift from their creator. This is confirmed by several stories, but none is as fascinating as the White Buffalo Calf Woman Lakota Legend.

The story begins with two young Lakota men who were given a very important task. They were asked to seek out the buffalos because the tribe didn't know where these animals lived.

So, the two young men were sent to explore the land on horseback. They couldn't have been riding an hour when they saw something approaching them from a great distance. They could see what it was, and because they thought that it might be a buffalo or another dangerous animal, they jumped into the nearby bushes to hide.

As they waited in their hiding place, they realized the figure approaching them was a beautiful woman. She carried a bundle of sage in her arms. She also saw

The two men realized that the figure approaching them was a beautiful woman.[19]

them as the bushes weren't thick enough to hide them. The woman stopped in front of the bush and looked at the two young men. They were enhanced by her beauty. One of them even said that he would like to marry the woman because she was the most beautiful one he had ever seen in his life. However, the other one said that the woman's beauty means she is holy and above ordinary people.

The woman heard the two men talking as she approached them even closer. When she was right in front of the bush, she put the bundle of sage she was carrying on the ground and beckoned the young men to come to her. She asked them what they wished for.

The man who said that he wanted to marry the woman immediately went to her and put his arms on hers, claiming her. Suddenly, the sky grew darker, and the wind picked up, creating a whirlwind and dust cloud, making the man and the woman disappear. Then, the wind quieted down, the dust settled, and the woman was standing where she was before. She was holding her sage bundle in her arms again, but the man disappeared. In his place, only a pile of bones was on the ground.

The other man wasn't frightened but stood in awe of this woman's power. Then, the woman told him she was going to visit his tribe. She urged Bull Walking Upright, a young Lakota guy, to return to his tribe and inform the others that she was on her way because she wanted to meet him.

She also instructed him to ask the other people to gather up and reposition their tents in a circle.

Additionally, they had to leave a gap in the circle pointing north. The woman concluded by saying that she intended to meet Bull Walking Upright at the largest tipi located in the circle's middle.

The young man hurried home and immediately recounted what the beautiful woman ordered. The others followed the directions and awaited her arrival. When the woman reached their camp, she had the sage bundle with her. Stepping into the circle, she revealed that she was hiding something under the bundle. She had brought a small pipe made of a vivid red stone as a present for the tribe. It has a buffalo's outline on it.

Bull Walking Upright was given the pipe by the woman, who also promised to teach him the proper prayers to offer to the Creator.

She told him that whenever he prays to the Creator for help, he must use the tiny pipe in the ceremony.

The woman also revealed that the pipe had a magical ability. When the tribe was hungry, they should lay out the pipe in the air, and it would summon the buffalos near their territory. This way, the hunters can provide food for their families.

The pipe would summon the buffalos near their territory.[20]

The woman had another lesson to teach the people. She explained to Bull Walking Upright that the earth that people live on is their mother. In order for everyone to live and use the Earth together peacefully, they need to respect Mother Earth and each other.

In addition, the woman instructed the tribe to dress like Mother Earth for ceremonies and taught them prayers they could recite to her.

They ought to dress in the hues that they can observe in nature, which are white, brown, red, and black. Furthermore, they would quickly discover that these hues match those of the buffalo.

Lastly, the beautiful woman reminded the tribe to always smoke the pipe before ceremonies and before creating a treaty. She said it would help bring peace because smoking the pipe would make everyone more peaceful. With a calmer mind, they could make better decisions and focus on asking for blessings from the Creator and Mother Nature. If they ask for something with the help of the pipe, they'll be sure to receive it.

After saying the last words, the beautiful woman turned, and stepping out of the circle, she slowly started to walk away while the tribe watched her in awe, their eyes shining with gratitude. She suddenly stopped and lay down on the ground. As she stood up, she transformed into a black buffalo cow. She rose like a red buffalo cow and lay down again. She changed into a brown buffalo cow when she lay down for the third time and into a white buffalo cow when she lay down for the fourth time.

The white buffalo then walked away from the people, disappearing over the hills in the north.

From this day on, Bull Walking Upright followed her directions. He kept the tiny red pipe with him wrapped up, only unwrapping it when it was time to gather the tribe and begin a ceremony. Before each lesson, he said the prayers the woman taught him.

Eventually, Bull Walking Upright grew old and too weak to hold ceremonies. He was over 100 years old and knew it was time to give the duty to another tribe member. He chose Sunrise — a wise man who was happy to learn the prayers and take the pipe. When it was time for him to step down, he again passed the pipe and the lessons to a worthy young tribe member, and so they have traveled down from many generations ever since. And, just as the woman promised, the pipe brought happiness and peace to the tribe.

Do you think the pipe made their community stronger? If so, how? What made this gift so powerful?

Have you ever received or given a gift that helped you become closer to someone?

The Story of How the Buffalo Hunt Began

The Plain Tribes were always known for their tight-knit community. [21]

The Plain Tribes were always known for their tight-knit community. In these warm communities, children did their chores obediently, the adults watched over them, and everyone looked out for each other.

Some were hunters and farmers, others warriors, and some did a little bit of everything. Some tribes moved around during the summer and winter but had a home to return to in the spring when they planted their crops and again in the fall when the crops were ready to harvest.

One of the activities that forged the Plain Tribe communities was hunting. They particularly liked hunting buffalos — and had lots of interesting ways to catch these large and powerful animals. For example, sometimes, they would chase them until the animal had to stop out of exhaustion. Others would pretend to be young buffalo crying desperately for help in order to lure an adult away from its herd.

Most tribes used the different parts of the buffalo for food, clothes, and other household items, once again involving the entire community in making these products.

However, according to their legends, the tribes didn't always hunt buffalo. The story of how the hunt for this magnificent animal began is a unique tale of community.

A long time ago, it wasn't the people who hunted the buffalo but the other way around. Buffalos — with the power of 20 bulls and a surprising speed of over 30 miles per hour — are moody creatures. They would attack and eat people if they were in a dark mood.

To keep the peace between people and buffalos, two birds — the hawk and the magpie — did their best to keep the animals away from people. However, this wasn't enough. Ultimately, they decided that all animals and people would enter a race, and the winners of this race could eat the losers!

Of course, the big and confident buffalos were happy to race, even though they knew that the course was a long trail around a dangerous mountain. Neika, the bravest of the buffalos, entered the race first.

The people were more cautious because they knew that they would get tired much faster. However, they had a plan for preventing fatigue from wearing them down and giving up before the finish line. After all, the stakes were high, and they risked being eaten by the buffalos and other scary animals. So, they set on to find a secret medicine that would make them strong enough to beat everyone else and reach the finish line first.

Meanwhile, all the other animals were preparing for the race, too. Some did this by painting themselves in vibrant colors. The magpie turned its tail, shoulders, and head white, and all the plain-looking animals maintained their bright coloring.

When everyone was ready, they lined up at the start line. Someone gave the signal, and the race was on. As they ran, Neika took the lead, with the magpie, the hawk, and the people behind her. The rest, like the slithering snakes, playful rabbits, buzzing insects, the cunning but not-quite-fast enough wolves, the diligent but tiny ants, and the other colorful birds, were following the leaders far behind. Despite their disadvantage, all animals tried encouraging themselves to run faster. The wolves howled, the insects beat their wings more quickly, the birds sang, and so on. It was undoubtedly a fascinating race to watch!

When they approached the mountainside, they picked up so much dust that no one was able to see each other, so they could only focus on themselves. The magpie and the hawk both knew that they could fly faster and catch up with Neika, but they chose to preserve their strengths until they were near the finish line. Then, they simply whooshed by Neika and won the race. As they made their circles of victory above the racecourse, they noticed that many animals had fallen. However, they were happy because they had no intention of eating anyone. They just wanted to help the people and stop the buffalos from hunting them.

When the two birds told the people that they had won the race in their name, they decided to start hunting and eating the buffalos. The buffalos heard this and ordered their young to hide to save them. However, before they allowed the youngsters to scurry away, they told them to take some of the leftover human flesh and put it in front of their chests. The young buffaloes did this and went to hide away as the people began their hunt. They spared the young ones until they grew up and then hunted them, too, using them all except for the bits of flesh in front of their chest. To this day, this part of the buffalo is not used because it's said to come from humans and not from animals.

When the two birds told the people that they had won the race in their name, they decided to start hunting and eating the buffalos. "

The people saw that none of the other animals were against them, so they spared every last one. They welcomed them into their lives, forming one big happy community. They only asked the birds for some of their fallen feathers to use for headpieces and other traditional decorations.

What do you think of the clever way the magpie and the hawk saved the people? And what about the people's decision to spare the other creatures and welcome them into their community?

Do you think it's important to welcome others into your life? Why?

True or False

Read the following sentences carefully. Some are true, others are not. Can you pick which ones are true?

- The Lakota didn't know where the buffalos lived.
- The beautiful woman said that she would bring a gift to the Lakota.
- The woman transformed four times, showing the four colors of the buffalo.
- The Lakota had forgotten about the pipe.
- People and the buffalos always lived in peace.
- The magpie and the hawk were on the side of the people.
- All the animals had vibrant colors on them before the race.
- The people started hunting buffalos after the race.

Chapter 5: Visions of Hope and Future: Prophecies

Many famous prophets have been predicting either a fascinating future or a bleak fate for generations. Like most other cultures and religions, the Native Americans also have prophets who show visions of both hope and doom. Many of their prophecies are centered on the latter, but interestingly, they also provide hope. Learning about them is like diving into a bottomless pit and finding your way back out unharmed.

The Hopi people belong to different tribes in northeastern Arizona, but most identify themselves with the Hopi Tribe of Arizona. [28]

The Hopi Prophecy

The Hopi people belong to different tribes in northeastern Arizona, but most identify themselves with the Hopi Tribe of Arizona. The Hopi Tribe is a sovereign nation in the United States, meaning it governs itself.

One of the most distinctive aspects of Hopi culture is its kachina religious practices. Spiritual creatures known as kachinas are thought to symbolize many facets of the natural world, spirits, and ancestors.

Hopi ceremonies involving kachinas are performed throughout the year to ensure the community's well-being, promote fertility, and bring rain for the crops to flourish. It is from one of these spiritual beings that the Hopi Prophecy originates.

According to their tradition, the Blue Star Kachina (also known as Saquasohuh) is said to represent the coming of the end of the world or a significant transition period (an apocalypse). Saquasohuh is a powerful spiritual being who will appear as a bright blue star in the sky — a moment that will herald major changes on Earth.

It doesn't refer to the blue stars that already exist in the night sky, like those in the Orion constellation. Many believe that Saquasohuh will be brighter than the brightest of the stars, and a few others say that it will be as huge as a mountain.

The arrival of this star is believed to bring purification and a spiritual awakening. This massive transformation won't necessarily be swift and calm. A few of the Hopi prophecies predict the appearance of the Red Star Kachina soon after Saquasohuh, which will result in destruction, chaos, and the end of the current world. It will be as big and bright as Saquasohuh.

However, just as they herald massive transformations and destruction, true to their Hopi prophecy name, they also give hope. This cleansing of the world can be avoided by maintaining harmony with nature and living under spiritual principles. These principles include:

- **Connection to Nature:** Many Native American spiritual beliefs emphasize a deep connection to the natural world. Nature is considered sacred, and humans are considered a part of, rather than separate from, the environment. Respect for all living beings and the Earth itself forms the foundation of their beliefs.

- **Harmony and Balance:** Balance is an essential concept in their spirituality. This includes finding balance within oneself and maintaining harmony with others and the natural world. Imbalance is often seen as the root of illness, conflict, and other problems.

They emphasize the interconnectedness of all things."

- **Interconnectedness:** They emphasize the interconnectedness of all things. "Things" is the keyword here. It doesn't simply imply the connection between humans but also their connection to the natural world, their ancestors, the spiritual realm, and everything else.

- **Respect for Elders and Ancestors:** Elders hold a special place in many Native American cultures, as they are valued for their wisdom, experience, and connection to tradition. Ancestors are also revered, and their guidance and protection are often sought through rituals and ceremonies, which brings the next point.

- **Ceremonies and Rituals:** Ceremonies and rituals play a significant role in spiritual practices. These may include rituals for healing, prayer, purification, rites of passage, and honoring the cycles of nature. These cycles include scientific ones like nitrogen and water and spiritual ones like birth and death.

Music, dance, and storytelling are the essence of their ceremonies, and they are known to use sacred objects like drums, feathers, and herbs to bring their ceremonies to fruition.

- **Spiritual Guardians and Guides:** They believe in the existence of spiritual guardians, guides, and helpers, but they aren't always immaterial or in the spiritual form. They may take the form of animal spirits, ancestors, or other beings who offer protection and assistance on the peoples' spiritual journey.

- **Respect for Diversity:** Their spiritual traditions recognize and honor the diversity of beliefs and practices among different tribes and individuals. There is no single absolute Native American religion — each tribe has its own unique spiritual teachings and practices.

- **Living in Harmony with Natural Cycles:** They emphasize the importance of living in accordance with the natural cycles of the earth, like the changing seasons and the cycles of the moon. This may involve practices such as planting and harvesting in harmony with the seasons or conducting ceremonies to mark significant celestial events.

In essence, the Hopi prophecy predicts doom but also provides solutions to prevent it from happening. Surprisingly, they are scientifically relevant. Over the years, human negligence of nature has made the threat of global warming a clear and present danger. It has become more than important to work toward environmental stewardship and spiritual renewal, which involves:

Many Native American tribes view the land as sacred and recognize their spiritual connection to it.[25]

- **A Sacred Relationship with the Land:** Many Native American tribes view the land as sacred and recognize their spiritual connection to it. They have a deep sense of responsibility and stewardship toward the environment, as the Earth is seen as a living entity deserving of reverence and protection.

- **Traditional Ecological Knowledge:** Indigenous peoples have accumulated generations of traditional ecological knowledge (TEK) about their local ecosystems, including plant and animal species, seasonal cycles, and sustainable resource management practices. This knowledge is passed down orally through storytelling, ceremonies, and everyday practices.

- **Sustainable Resource Use:** They have been historically practicing sustainable resource use, harvesting only what is necessary and ensuring that resources are replenished for future generations. Traditional hunting, fishing, agriculture, and gathering techniques involve careful observation of ecological patterns and cycles to avoid overexploitation.

- **Conservation Practices:** They have developed numerous conservation practices to preserve biodiversity and maintain healthy ecosystems. These include controlled burning to manage forests, rotating agricultural fields to prevent soil depletion, and creating protected areas for wildlife.

- **Ritual Practices:** Many Native American ceremonies and rituals are dedicated to honoring the Earth and its natural cycles. They involve prayers, offerings, and symbolic gestures to express gratitude for the gifts of the land and to ask for guidance in living harmoniously with nature.

- **Environmental Advocacy:** Indigenous peoples have been at the forefront of environmental advocacy (support) efforts locally and globally. Many tribes have fought to protect their ancestral lands from environmental degradation caused by extractive industries, pollution, and unsustainable development. They are known to advocate for the recognition of land rights and the incorporation of indigenous knowledge into conservation efforts.

- **Community-Based Approaches:** Environmental stewardship is often community-driven, with decision-making processes guided by traditional values, consensus-building, and collective responsibility. This approach lends a strong sense of solidarity and collaboration in protecting the environment for future generations.

This prophecy signifies that nature is a powerful force with the potential to make or break the world. If it's taken care of, it will build a sustainable future for all the living beings on this planet, but if it's misused, it will transform into a force of death and destruction by inviting Saquasohuh (the Blue Star Kachina) into the skies. In short, caring for all natural things is critical for preventing the Hopi prophecy from coming to fruition.

The Seventh Generation Prophecy

It is a fact that Native Americans are at the forefront of battling environment-harming practices.[36]

It is a fact that Native Americans are at the forefront of battling environment-harming practices, and this drive primarily arises from the Seventh Generation Prophecy. It is a concept deeply rooted in the spiritual beliefs of many indigenous peoples in the U.S. While it varies among different tribes and nations, the prophecy generally emphasizes the connections between generations and the responsibility of present-day actions to future generations – going about seven generations into the future!

The origins of the Seventh Generation Prophecy can be traced back to various Native American oral traditions and teachings. Among some tribes, it is believed that decisions made by the current generation should be guided by their impact on the well-being of the seventh generation yet to come.

For instance, if a person is about to decide their career, they should consider its impact on seven generations of people after them. Suppose they are considering engineering as their career. In that case, they should try to make a difference that would benefit seven generations down the line. The same goes for painting, agriculture, science, and virtually anything else. This concept underscores the importance of sustainability, stewardship of the land, and the preservation of cultural values and traditions.

Key aspects of the Seventh Generation Prophecy include:

- It emphasizes the interconnectedness of all living beings and the recognition that actions taken today have consequences that reverberate through future generations. It reflects a holistic worldview that acknowledges the complex web of relationships between humans, nature, and the spiritual realm.

- It underscores the responsibility of the present generation to act as stewards of the Earth and its resources. This involves making decisions that put future generations' long-term well-being over short-term gains and ensuring the sustainability of natural ecosystems and cultural practices. For example, suppose an engineer can make quick bucks out of a project that will potentially harm the region's future. In that case, they will reject it and make sure that it doesn't become a reality.

- In addition to environmental stewardship, the prophecy often emphasizes the importance of preserving cultural traditions, languages, and knowledge systems. This includes passing down ancestral teachings and wisdom to successive generations and ensuring the continuity of indigenous cultures and identities.

- One of the prime beliefs goes something like this: the Seventh Generation Prophecy is guided by spiritual forces and ancestral wisdom. Ceremonies, prayers, and rituals may be conducted to seek guidance and blessings for the future and to honor the spirits of ancestors who have come before and those who are yet to come. It is more like shaping the future through the wisdom of history.

- It has inspired indigenous communities to advocate for (actively support and push for) social and environmental justice and recognize Native American rights and sovereignty. Activism efforts often center on issues like land rights, environmental conservation, and cultural revitalization, focusing on creating a better world for future generations.

Overall, the Seventh Generation Prophecy is a guiding principle for Native American culture, shaping their worldview, values, and actions about the past, present, and future. It highlights the importance of living in harmony with the Earth and each other and the deep connections that bind all generations.

The world may be spiraling out of control today. But, the prophecy provides the hope of a rising generation that will restore the balance between humans and the natural world, symbolizing a renewal of values and a return to ancestral wisdom.

The Create-Your-Own-Prophecy Exercise

Prophecies are meant to be predicted – and everyone guesses about an outcome from time to time. Will your favorite sports team win? Will it rain today?

Before this exercise, please ask a parent or guardian if they agree with you doing it – and remind them that it is just for fun!

While Native American shamans are very serious about their prophecies, this exercise is only designed for you to consider the steps involved in making a heartfelt guess about something. Your hopes and dreams for the world are important to you, and giving them some thought can be a fun exercise.

Take a pen and paper (or chalk and a blackboard if you have them) and write down how the world is *right now*. For instance, when this book was written, the coronavirus (COVID-19) had lessened a lot – but it and other diseases still plague many parts of the globe. There is a fierce war going on between Russia and Ukraine, another war between Israel and its enemies, and economies worldwide are in turmoil. (You can Google every prominent problem the world faces at this moment.)

1. Write down how the world should be ***instead of how it is***. Should all the wars end? Should the coronavirus stop existing?
    o Should there be harmony between all the nations in the world?
    o Could humans learn to live with nature instead of destroying it?
    o How about including technology as a means of joy and harmony?

Consider how the world needs to be instead of doing all the harmful things it is doing. Write down how you see the world COULD BE in the future.

2. Discuss your desires with family and friends. What do they think about the predictions? Do they have any ideas about how to arrive at a better future?

3. Draw a simple picture of how things would be if your predictions and hopes came true. About the environment, perhaps you draw a picture of a girl hugging an oak tree. A boy playing with his pet dog might show a love for animals. The ending of a war could be a picture of different people hugging instead of fighting.

While we can leave true prophesying to prophets and shamans, you can learn a lot about yourself by guessing how the world might be a better place.

Chapter 6: Celebrating Nature

The wind blew gently, like someone speaking softly in Muata's ear. It carried the earthy smell of ancient trees and dirt. Sunlight peeked through the leaves above, making flickering shapes dance on the ground like sunlight on water. The young boy wasn't just standing in the forest; he felt completely surrounded by it. It was like a world that was alive, full of secrets waiting to be discovered.

Muata wasn't just standing in any ordinary forest. For generations, their people had walked hand-in-hand with this ancient place. Here, whispers of the past lingered in the rustling leaves. Elders spoke of spirits who waltzed in crackling firelight, their wisdom carried on the wind. Powerful creatures, guardians of the mountains, were more than just bedtime stories – they were the very essence of this land. Respecting it wasn't a duty; it was a thrilling pact. Understanding its rhythms was an adventure on its own, waiting to be unraveled. Living in harmony with nature meant they weren't just focused on surviving; this was how they lived their lives. To the Native Americans, nature is like a living legend, waiting to be embraced by those brave enough to listen.

To the Native Americans, nature is like a living legend, waiting to be embraced by those brave enough to listen. "

The morning sun had a mischievous glint in its eye as it peeked through the ancient trees. It stood high in the sky, painting patterns on Muata's worn leather satchel. Today wasn't just any day. Today, the forest hummed with a promise whispered in the wind. The boy was so excited, and anticipation bubbled in the boy's chest like a hidden spring!

In his hand, his trusty sketchbook felt less like paper and more like a portal, which was about to be filled with the magic his Grandma would unleash through stories. They weren't just stories to be heard – they were an invitation, a chance to peek behind the veil of everyday life and see the extraordinary. Today, Muata would be listening to tales of the forest's power and the animals' wisdom; he'd become part of them; his heart was a blank page ready to be inscribed with the reverence his people held for this incredible world. With each skip along the familiar path, the forest floor crunched under his eager steps, and the very Earth seemed to beckon him deeper into the waiting wonder.

Finally, Grandma's cottage came into sight from the forest's emerald embrace. Smoke curled from its chimney, promising warmth and the comforting scent of woodsmoke and freshly baked bread. As Muata burst through the weathered wooden door, a wave of familiar warmth washed over him. The air hummed with the gentle hum of the old rocking chair by the fireplace, and the room was bathed in a golden glow emanating from the crackling fire.

There, nestled in her tiny cot by the hearth, sat Grandma. Her face, etched with the wisdom of years spent in communion with the land, cradled a warm smile as she saw him. Her eyes sparkled with the promise of an adventure waiting to unfold. Muata's heart thumped a happy rhythm. He scrambled across the worn wooden floor, his satchel clutched tightly in his hand and settled himself onto the small stool beside her cot. He was ready. The tales of some legends were waiting, and Grandma held the key.

Grandma's voice, raspy with age yet strangely captivating, filled the room, weaving a spell with each word. The older woman cleared her throat and started with a smile on her face.

The Raven and the Stolen Light – A Tlingit Legend

There was a raven called Kit-ka'ositiyi-qa-yit, which means "Son of Kit-ka'ositiyi-qa." *

"Sit still, little one," she began, her eyes twinkling like distant stars. "Let me tell you a tale of a time before time. In the beginning, there was a being called Raven. He was called Kit-ka'ositiyi-qa-yit, which means "Son of Kit-ka'ositiyi-qa." After several tries, he created the world, but it was a blanket of endless nights. Not a single star dared peek, and not a sliver of moon was anywhere to be seen. Darkness, thick as bear fur, clung to everything."

She paused, taking a sip from a steaming mug held in her hands. Muata leaned in, anticipation buzzing in his veins.

Her voice dropped to a whisper, sending shivers down Muata's spine. "There was a powerful guardian – a grumpy fellow. He was living in a large house far up the hill. He had a cold heart. The guardian kept the stars, moon, and even the sun locked away in a box, jealously keeping the light for himself." She shook her head.

"Our people were lost, groping and fumbling in the dark because of the guardian's greed. Raven, bless his clever soul, couldn't bear to see their plight. He was never one to shy away from a challenge, so it didn't take long for him to devise a cunning trick. So, he hatched a plan – a daring one that would forever change the face of the world."

"This grumpy guardian, he had a daughter. And what did Raven do? He shrunk himself down to be smaller than a teardrop. Mmhmmm. He turned himself into something as tiny as dirt and jumped into the woman's favorite glass cup. She drank of the cup and became pregnant." Grandma chuckled. Muata's eyes widened, picturing the trickster in his mind.

"When Raven grew into a babe, he found the shelf where the guardian kept his treasures. The baby, him being Raven in disguise, of course, cried for everything he could see. "Shiny!" he'd yell, pointing at the objects stacked high in the corner for three days. Each day, when the guardian couldn't take the wailing any longer, he brought down those boxes and gave them to the lad just to quiet the little Raven down one by one."

Raven let out the stars. ³⁹

Grandma's eyes gleamed with amusement. "What do you think Raven did with the boxes, Muata? He first let out the stars and then the moon up the smoke hole. They both shot into the sky before anyone could blink. But, the Raven kept the last box with himself for a while after escaping."

"One day, he heard of a man who guarded a well with abundant water, so he decided to trick him as well. He turned himself into the man's brother-in-law and drank all the water until it was almost finished. He tried to escape when the man caught him but got stuck in the smoke hole. The man got angry, so he made a fire under the Raven while he hung in the smoke hole, unable to fly away. All that smoke from his fire turned Raven's feathers black as night."

"Raven finally escaped, spitting water here and there. That was how he created the great rivers of the world. He landed in a village, but the villagers tried to fight him for the last box that he had, so he opened the box, and the sun shot up into the sky. And, so our people were bathed in glorious light, a gift from the cleverest trickster the world had ever known."

She winked at Muata, a knowing glint in her eye. "So, you see, little one, even the smallest creature can hold the greatest courage. And sometimes, a little trickery can bring about the most beautiful light."

Glooscap and the Changing Seasons (A Mi'kmaq Tale)

"Muata, scoot closer and let the firelight warm you up," his grandma said. "I have another tale for you." She adjusted herself in her chair.

"Long, long ago, in the land of the Mi'kmaq people, there, a mighty spirit named Glooscap roamed. He had great strength and wisdom. But, even Glooscap couldn't hold back the god of winter who sought to freeze the world." Muata's eyes widened. His grandma nodded, "Yes, indeed."

"One day, the crystal teeth of frost bit into the earth, turning colorful forests into brittle statues and rivers into ice. The Mi'kmaq people cried out. Glooscap's heart was heavy with the people's

The Mi'kmaq people believed that a mighty spirit named Glooscap roamed their land. [80]

sorrow – he wouldn't give in. He kept fighting frost to frost with the god of winter until he could no longer do so."

"With a roar that shook the very mountains, he set off to find the god of summer – the spirit chased away by the god of winter's icy fist. His journey was long and harsh. But, Glooscap pushed on – his determination etching lines on his face, his eyes burning with the promise of spring."

"Finally, after a very long and difficult trip, Glooscap reached the god of summer's land. It was warm there, sunshine everywhere, unlike the freezing cold he'd just been in. He found Summer relaxing under beautiful flowers, wearing a crown made of sunlight." "When he spoke, Glooscap's voice was rough from the cold. He told the god of summer about the Mi'kmaq people and how the god of winter had made their land all icy. Glooscap's voice showed how much he cared about his people, and he really wanted things to be normal again with the four seasons."

"The god of summer saw how upset Glooscap was and felt bad for him. He stood up and smiled kindly. He was touched by Glooscap's bravery and humility. Then, he, the god of summer, waved his hand, and the cold winter chill disappeared. A soft wind blew across Mi'kma'ki, and the first spring flowers started to bloom, melting away the frost. The four seasons were back in order, just like before, all thanks to Glooscap's bravery."

These stories remind us that nature is so much more than just the ground we walk on. [81]

These stories remind us that nature is so much more than just the ground we walk on. It's like one big, living storybook filled with lessons and adventures scattered across the pages within. The Raven's cleverness showed how we should be confident in ourselves. Even the smallest person can make a big impact. Glooscap's journey taught us the importance of balance and respect for the changing seasons. Like both of these legends, we can build a special connection with nature even by simply stepping outside and feeling the sunshine on our faces. Amazing things happen all around us every single day. So, next time you're feeling curious, step outside, explore, and celebrate the incredible world we share with all living things.

Activity

Nature Appreciation Journal

Are you ready to take your love for nature to the next level? Grab your hat and sunscreen – we're going outside to see the wonders of nature!

What Is a Nature Appreciation Journal?

It serves as a place to record all of your outside senses—hearing, seeing, smelling, and feeling.

Did you find a feathery surprise that a squirrel left behind? Did the wind whisper secrets through the leaves? Jot it all down!

1. **Step 1:** Find a notebook you like, colorful or plain, big or small. Something you can write and draw in.

2. **Step 2:** Grab your favorite pencils, markers, crayons, or paints. If you like drawing outside, bring a clipboard or something hard to write on.

3. **Step 3:** Lace up those hiking boots and head outside, whether in your backyard or a nearby park. Take a deep breath and soak in the sights, sounds, and smells of nature all around you.

4. **Step 4:** Take a closer look. Pay attention to everything around you. See the shapes of leaves, the colors of flowers, and how tree bark feels. Listen to birds chirping, leaves blowing, and maybe even a stream trickling. Feel the wind, smell the dirt after a rain, and listen to all the sounds around you.

5. **Step 5:** Use your paper and pencil. To let everyone around you know what you experienced, record in writing or drawing everything you saw, heard, smelled, tasted, and felt.

Write about animals, plants, or places you saw. Draw pictures, write poems, stories, or how you felt about being outside. Set your imagination free.

6. **Step 6:** Observe the changes that happen over time. Return to the same spot outside and see how it changes with the seasons. Look for spring flowers, summer leaves, pretty fall colors, etc.

7. **Step 7:** As you spend time outdoors and fill your journal with your own unique observations and creations, take a moment to reflect on your experiences. How did it feel to connect with nature on a deeper level? What did you learn about yourself and the world around you?

8. **Step 8:** Your discoveries are not meant for your eyes alone. Once you've filled your nature appreciation journal with all your amazing observations and experiences, share your findings with the people around you. Sharing your journal is not only a way to connect with friends, family, or classmates, but it's also an opportunity to inspire each other to explore and appreciate the wonders of nature even more.

9. **Step 9:** Keep exploring, observing, and filling your nature appreciation journal with discoveries and insights. With each new adventure, you'll deepen your connection with nature and gain a greater appreciation for its stories and lessons.

So, what are you waiting for? Grab your journal and head outside to embark on your next great adventure. Allow nature to teach you its ways, and the world will become your personal playground.

Chapter 7: Trickster Tales

Native American tales aren't all about magic, nature, and spiritual ancestors. They are a collection of fascinating trickster tales that have people laughing their heads off while learning a useful thing or two. They are stories of cunningness, wisdom, bravery, and stupidity, but they also give you unexpected morals you can live by. It's time to outsmart the smartest tricksters in Native American folklore and learn a few good things in the process.

The Coyote and the Rattlesnake

A lone coyote feeling refreshed after having a drink at the pool. [53]

A rattlesnake is considered to be the wisest of the wise. [38]

As far as the eye can see, the landscape stretched out into an endless expanse of barrenness. The Earth was a tapestry of shifting sands, ranging in color from golden yellows to deep reds, moving up and down in graceful curves and dunes sculpted by the relentless winds.

The sky above was a brilliant blue, uninterrupted by clouds for days on end. The sun beat down relentlessly on the rolling sands and (surprisingly) the considerable patches of vegetation that had sustained wildlife in the arid region for generations. A sheet of water reflecting the blue sky glimmered blissfully in the distance, and just beyond that, a row of snow-capped peaks were faintly visible, lining the expanse.

Despite the beauty of the desert and the unexpected sources of food and water available, a lone coyote could be seen ambling up a large dune, feeling refreshed after having a drink at the pool. No other animals were visible for miles around, at least on the surface.

A multitude of lizards were nestled in their hidey holes beneath the sand, their worn-out scales craving for a bit of sun and water. Snakes slithered through the underbrush, their sinuous forms disappearing into the shadows. Birds of prey were seen as indiscernible dots on the horizon, never daring to circle near the coyote.

Who was this coyote that formidable creatures like lizards, snakes, and vultures preferred to hide from rather than come near him? He wasn't a fearsome beast but looked more like a frailer, smaller version of a wolf. He barely had any sharp teeth or claws. His fur was decaying, and his body had lost its original strength. He was getting old, after all.

However, the coyote's eyes sparkled with cunningness and malice. Indeed, it was his brain and wit that made him the most intimidating animal in the land. He was the sliest of the sly, outsmarting anyone and everyone who crossed his path and stealing their most prized possessions.

All living creatures in the beautiful desert had learned to avoid him like the plague, including humans, the apex predator, and the most intelligent of all animals.

"It seemed not all creatures had learned their lesson," the coyote thought, for when he reached the top of the dune, he could see something slither toward him over the sand below – someone whose head glittered in the afternoon sun. As it crawled nearer, he could see it was a snake holding a dazzling golden gem on its head.

"Ha, another snake!" thought the coyote. He seemed new in the desert. "Look at him flaunting his shiny gem. It's mesmerizing and beautiful. I want it. I'll have it. Let him come!"

However, the slithering creature, now climbing the dune on which the coyote stood, wasn't just any snake. He was a rattlesnake, considered to be the wisest of the wise, whom nobody had managed to outsmart so far. But he was also kind, compassionate, and quick to forgive.

The coyote didn't know all this, and when the rattlesnake arrived at the top, the sly old animal greeted him with a fake smile: "How are you, my dear friend? What is that thing on your head?"

"I'm good. Thank you for asking, friend," the rattlesnake replied. "I came all the way from those snow-covered mountains beyond the lake. Oh, and this is my precious gem – a symbol of knowledge and power."

"It's magnificent!" the coyote said with a hint of greed. Quickly realizing it, he tried to cover it up by saying, "Come now. You must be tired after the long journey. Unload your burden and take some rest in the shadow of this dune on the other side."

"Thank you, I will. I'll leave the gem buried just beneath the sand here so it doesn't attract greedy eyes. Will you stand guard over it, please?"

"I'll guard it with my life!" the coyote promised eagerly.

"Thank you! You're too kind," said the rattlesnake gratefully. Then, he dug up a small part of the sand, placed his gem in the hollow, and covered it up with the surrounding sand again. Crawling to the other side of the dune, he slept soundly in its shadow.

The coyote couldn't contain his excitement. "This was too easy," he thought. "I didn't even need to use my cunningness. Fool of a snake. I'll take really good care of his gem, back in my cave. But first, I need to make sure he is asleep."

He crept down to where the rattlesnake lay and closely monitored his breathing. After a couple of hours, his breathing stabilized as he began to snore. The coyote crept back up the slope and greedily started digging the sand in the exact spot where the gem lay buried.

Several minutes passed, but he couldn't see the sparkling gem. "This is strange," he thought. "The foolish snake hadn't buried it too deep." To the west, the sun was about to set, but he kept digging, getting more and more impatient. Minutes turned to hours, and the small hollow became a large hole on top of the dune, but he still hadn't found the precious gem.

It was dark outside, and the hole was getting deeper, but the coyote had eyes only for the gem, so he continued to dig. Finally, he reached hard ground beneath the sand, and he could dig no further. That was when he decided to give up, thinking the gem was lost.

For the first time since he had begun digging, he looked up. Night had turned to day, but he could only see a tiny dot of the morning sky above; that was how deep he had dug himself. He tried to climb up, but he couldn't get a grip on the towering wall of sand. It kept slipping from his paws.

Just as he was about to give up and resign himself to his fate, he noticed a dark spot in the opening above. It was the head of the snake he had tried to dupe. He shouted up to him, "Help!"

"Why did you dig a hole so deep? Were you trying to find my gem?" The rattlesnake asked.

The coyote sheepishly replied, "Yes."

"Did you find it?"

"No."

The snake chuckled, and his head vanished from the opening. The coyote was afraid. Was the snake so angry with him that he had left him to rot in the hole? As dark thoughts consumed him, the snake's head popped in the opening again. This time, there wasn't just one but a dozen heads looking down at the coyote.

They were all the snakes he had outsmarted and stolen from in the desert. They were coiling their heads and tails around each other, and within moments, they had formed a long rope of snakes. The coyote gave a sigh of relief when the foremost snake who jumped in the hole (dragging the others down) was able to reach the bottom.

The rattlesnake was the last one holding the rest from above, and when the coyote held tight to the bottommost snake, he pulled the makeshift rope and dragged everyone up to the surface. When the coyote was out of the hole, he stammered his thanks to everyone and said to the rattlesnake, "I'm sorry I tried to take your gem and for losing it, too."

The rattlesnake tricked the coyote with a piece of ice crystal that he carved from a cave.[u]

The rattlesnake laughed and said, "Oh, but it was never a gem to begin with. It was just a piece of ice crystal I had carved from a cave in those snow-capped mountains. If you weren't so consumed by greed when you first saw it and took me for a fool, you might have noticed the water trailing off its sides as it slowly melted from the heat.

"Your sinister reputation had reached us animals up there. I knew you would try to take the gem at the first opportunity. By the time you started digging for it, it had completely melted into water, so you found nothing there. Any normal animal would have left it at that, but your greed prompted you to dig yourself deeper into the hole."

Indeed, the outsmarter was outsmarted. At the same time, the coyote was humbled. He realized that true wisdom lies in knowing that others are equally wise. Despite their grievances, the other snakes came to help him, which made him respect every living creature. The experience transformed the cunning trickster into a wise animal.

The Raven's Moonlit Dance

Many of the Native American tribes believe the coyote to be the trickster, but the majority of them hail the raven as the god of tricks.

The majority of the Native American tribes hail the raven as the god of tricks. [85]

A mischievous raven lived in the heart of the dense forest, where the moon's silver light dances through the leaves. He was known far and wide for his cunning ways and his insatiable desire for beauty. He often dreamed of attending the grand forest gathering, where creatures from all corners of the woods would gather to celebrate the full moon.

On a full moon night, as he perched atop a mighty oak, he gazed at his plain black feathers and longed for the colorful hues of the other birds. Determined to stand out at the gathering, he devised a cunning plan. He would adorn himself with the most exquisite feathers stolen from his fellow birds.

He flew from tree to tree, charming his way into the birds' trust with sweet words and promises of friendship. And, one by one, he plucked feathers from their plumage, leaving behind a trail of betrayal and sorrow.

Adorned with feathers of every color imaginable, the raven made his way to the grand gathering, his heart swelling with pride at the sight of his magnificent disguise. But, as he entered the clearing, he was met with whispers and stares of disapproval from the other creatures.

Undeterred, he strutted into the gathering, eager to bask in the admiration of his peers. But, as the night unfolded, he began to feel a sense of unease creeping into his heart. Despite his elaborate disguise, he couldn't shake the feeling of emptiness that gnawed at his soul.

As the hours passed and the moon reached its zenith, he found himself drawn to a quiet corner of the clearing where a wise old owl sat in silent contemplation. Intrigued, the raven approached the creature.

"What ails you, raven?" the owl asked, fixing him with a knowing gaze.

"I sought to be admired and celebrated, but instead, I feel only shame and regret," the raven confessed sadly.

The wise owl revealed that true beauty lies in the authenticity of our hearts. [86]

The owl nodded and spread his wings to reveal his glory. "True beauty lies not in the adornments we wear but in the authenticity of our hearts," he said softly. "You are a creature of the night, raven, and your true beauty shines brightest when you embrace your own nature."

With a heavy heart, the raven realized the folly of his vanity. He returned to his nest in the cliffs and shed his stolen feathers. That moonlit night, he had found a new sense of freedom in his authenticity as he began to accept himself the way he was. He soared across the heavens, spreading his black wings, knowing that true beauty could only be found in the depths of one's own heart.

Two Truths and a Lie

Each question below is based on the two stories above. Each question has three options — two are true, and one is a lie. Choose the lie to score points!

1. Which animals were in the desert?

- Lizards
- Foxes
- Snakes

2. Who hid from the coyote?

- Lizards
- Vultures
- Snakes

Hint: They didn't come near the coyote, but they weren't exactly hiding from him.

3. What did the coyote want from the rattlesnake?

- He wanted the rattlesnake's head.
- He wanted to outsmart the rattlesnake.
- He wanted the rattlesnake's gem.

4. What was the moral of the coyote's story?

- To respect every living creature
- The wise were those who considered everyone wise
- To know that vanity is a folly

5. What was the raven known for?

- His insatiable desire for beauty
- His wisdom
- His cunningness

6. **What did the owl say to the raven?**
   - True beauty lies in the adornments we wear.
   - True beauty shines brightest upon embracing one's nature.
   - True beauty is in the authenticity of our hearts.

7. **What did the raven do after going back to his nest?**
   - Shed his stolen feathers
   - Spread his black wings
   - Failed to realize his folly

Chapter 8: The Whispering Winds: Stories of Adventure

The Native Americans have been adoring, worshiping, and living in nature for eons, and with nature comes adventure. Their tales are far different, more thrilling, unimaginably magical, and even more adventurous than the regular adventure stories of other civilizations. Their folklore unravels many mysteries of nature and embodies the spirit of exploration and bravery in the unlikeliest of places.

The Native Americans have been adoring, worshiping, and living in nature for eons. [87]

The Journey of Falling Star

In some Native American tales, Falling Star refers to a legendary figure who fell from the heavens to save the world from falling into chaos. In others, he is a young warrior blessed with the spirit of the wild and the wisdom of his ancestors. In every story, however, he is a curious hero with a thirst for adventure.

One of the tales portrayed a unique natural world where forests were as old as the Earth and mountains touched the sky. The ever-flowing waters of the rivers showed the dazzling beauty of their depths, and all animals, birds, and insects existed in perfect harmony with each other.

In such a wonderful world, there lived a young warrior named Falling Star. He was renowned not only for his skill in battle but also for his deep love for nature and his unquenchable thirst for knowledge. However, he didn't venture far from the confines of the forest where he lived, not for lack of curiosity, but because he loved his family even more.

One evening, as he sat beneath a large oak with his eyes closed, listening to the gentle rustle of leaves and the distant calls of night owls, an elder interrupted his reverie to share a tale of a legendary flower.

"There is a flower of wisdom that is said to bloom only once every hundred years. Tomorrow marks its day of blooming."

"What is so special about this flower apart from the hundred-year blooming period?" asked Falling Star. "Is it beautiful to behold? Does it have a captivating smell?"

The flower of wisdom is said to bloom only once every hundred years. [38]

"It is all that and more," replied the elder. "Rumors abound that whoever possesses its petals will be granted unparalleled wisdom and a singular insight into how the world works."

Falling Star was fascinated by the prospect of such vast knowledge, and his family encouraged him to seek the flower. He had finally found his calling, and amid many tearful goodbyes and promises to return with the flower, he embarked on a quest to find it. With his trusty blade at his side and a determined heart, he ventured into the unknown.

His journey led him through dense forests where the trees were as old as time itself, and the trickling streams held water so pure that their flow created a sweet melody. Each step brought new challenges, from treacherous ravines to slippery cliffs. Yet, he also encountered friendly faces, as a great white stag helped him back on the right path when he took a wrong turn, and an enigmatic owl accompanied him in the dead of night.

As he ascended the rugged slopes of towering mountains, battling fierce winds and biting cold, Falling Star marveled at the majesty of the world around him. At first, he was daunted by the tall peaks shrouded in clouds and the sheer extremity of the elements (heavy rains that felt like hailstorms and fierce winds that almost swept him over the edge of cliffs). Eventually, he learned to respect the raw power of nature, finding beauty in its harshest landscapes and wisdom in its untamed wilderness.

Through perseverance and determination, he finally reached the summit of the tallest peak, where legend spoke of the magical flower's hidden sanctuary. There, amid a carpet of colorful blooms and crystalline waters, he beheld the fabled flower, its petals glowing with an ethereal light.

With trembling hands, Falling Star plucked a single petal, feeling a surge of ancient wisdom course through his veins. It was like he was holding the weight of the entire world in his hands, yet it felt as light as a feather. At that moment, he understood the true meaning of knowledge – not as a prize to be won but a journey to be embraced. It was an unquenchable thirst that needed to be filled from time to time, just like a water bottle.

Falling Star's journey taught him the value of perseverance and respect for nature. [80]

As he descended from the mountain, cradling the precious petal close to his heart, Falling Star quietly reflected on his journey. His quest had granted him a deeper insight into the natural world. It had taught him the value of perseverance, respect for nature, and the boundless power of the human spirit to seek knowledge in the face of unprecedented dangers. And, though his journey had ended, and he was about to return home, his quest for knowledge would continue.

Echoes of the Canyon

It is said that the whispers of the wind carry echoes of the past, voices of Native American ancestors that reverberate across massive mountain ranges and deep canyons. One such tale narrates the adventure of a young girl named Whispering Wind.

In the quiet expanse of a forgotten forest, where sunlight streamed and twinkled through the trees and the wind whistled over the grass, there lived a young girl named Whispering Wind. She was unlike the other children of her village – her eyes always alight with curiosity and her spirit as wild as the wind itself.

Every evening, her grandmother told her tales of history and adventure, of her ancestors and the natural world at the beginning of time. Unfortunately, there came a time when she had exhausted all her stories and didn't have any new ones to tell. Seeing the dejected look on Whispering Wind's face, she said, "Legend says there is a hidden canyon south of here that echoes with voices of the past. It never runs out of fantastical tales which also happen to be true."

Legend says there is a hidden canyon south of here that echoes with voices of the past. ⁴⁰

"Won't it be dangerous? They sound like ghosts," said Whispering Wind apprehensively.

"The unknown speaks of dangers untold. Can your curiosity overcome your fear?"

"I don't know."

"Then, go find out."

And so, Whispering Wind ventured southward, deeper into the forest than she had ever gone before. The trees were so thick that barely any sunlight trickled through. It was always dark as the night, but still, she plodded on. The path, which she could hardly see, was winding and treacherous. She stumbled and fell several times, but she got back up each time and continued her journey.

After several days that seemed like years, she arrived at the edge of a wide canyon. It stretched before her like a yawning chasm, its depths shrouded in a thick fog and an even thicker mystery. Despite its daunting presence, she felt an irresistible pull drawing her closer, beckoning her to explore its secrets.

With each step she took, the air seemed to hum with the echoes of a thousand voices . . . faint whispers carried on the breeze. Whispering Wind may have braved the dangerous path that led her there, but she was too afraid to carry on any further. Nevertheless, her curiosity took the better of her, and she longed to know what the voices were saying. The echoes felt like an enchanting melody of knowledge and history that soothed all her fears and gave her courage. Eventually, she descended into the depths of the canyon, her heart pounding with excitement.

As she ventured deeper, the whispers grew louder and clearer, swirling around her like a whirlwind of memories. With each passing moment, she felt herself being transported back in time to a world where her ancestors roamed the land and their stories echoed through the ages.

"He was a gifted horse trainer who tamed the wildest beasts..."

"She was a fierce warrior against whom the strongest men felt weak..."

Whispering Wind listened with rapt attention as the voices of the past filled the canyon, narrating a tapestry of tales that spanned generations. There was a group of brave warriors who fought valiantly to protect their people, wise elders who passed down ancient wisdom, and bold adventurers who explored uncharted territories in search of new land.

But, amid the tales of heroism and triumph, she also heard whispers of sorrow and loss – of battles fought and lives sacrificed in the name of freedom and justice. And, with each story she heard, she gained a deeper understanding of the struggles and hardships that had shaped her heritage.

Despite the dark nature of some of the tales, Whispering Wind felt a sense of pride and honor for the legacy that had been passed down to her. She experienced her ancestors' courage and resilience course through her veins, guiding her forward as she walked the path they had paved before her.

As the sun was about to set, casting a dull glow across the canyon walls, Whispering Wind climbed back up from the depths with a newfound sense of purpose. She knew that she carried with her the stories of her ancestors, their wisdom, courage, losses, and triumphs – her history, in short.

Her journey back home was spent in profound reflection. She realized that the echoes of the hidden canyon may have been ghosts, but she was no longer afraid of them. If anything, she felt closer to her family's heritage and traditions. She knew she was no longer just a girl wandering through the forest – she had become a guardian of that heritage, a keeper of the stories that had shaped her identity.

Armed with the power of history, she was ready to face whatever challenges lay ahead. "

As she looked out at the world stretching before her, she knew that she was ready to face whatever challenges lay ahead, armed with the power of history, the curiosity that had led her to the mystical place, and the unwavering belief in the value of self-discovery. In the echoes of the past, Whispering Wind had found her roots and the strength to do good things and accomplish great wonders in the future. For one, she would be telling stories to her grandmother, not the other way around.

Create Your Own Adventure Story

Adventure stories are highly inspirational. They motivate people not just to go for an adventure of their own but also to create their own adventure story. This simple activity only requires a notebook, a pen, imagination, and a thirst for adventure. Here's an example to start with:

Once upon a time, in the heart of a forest, there lived a young boy. His village was in the middle of a vast clearing, surrounded by all kinds of trees and wildlife.

One day, his grandfather called him to his hut and told him of a sacred totem hidden deep within the forest. He said that it was the key to unlocking the wisdom of their ancestors.

Prompt 1: The Journey Begins

Accompanied by his loyal wolf companion, the young boy set out on his quest to find the sacred totem. Along the way, he encountered a gushing river blocking his path. How does he overcome this obstacle?

Prompt 2: Trial of the Forest Spirits

As he went deeper into the forest, he stumbled upon mysterious spirits dancing in the moonlight. To proceed, he must prove his worthiness by completing a task. What challenges do they present to him?

Prompt 3: Encounter with the Wise Owl

Guided by the whispers of the wind, the young boy came upon a wise old owl perched high in the branches of an ancient oak tree. The owl offered him cryptic advice that would aid him on his journey. What is that advice?

Prompt 4: The Guardians of the Sacred Totem

At long last, he reached the heart of the forest where the sacred totem lay. But, before he could claim it, he must face the guardians – spirits of the ancestors tasked with protecting their legacy. How does he prove himself worthy of their trust?

Prompt 5: The Return Home

With the sacred totem in hand, the young boy embarked on the journey back to his village, where his grandfather awaited his return. Along the way, he reflected on the lessons he learned and the challenges he overcame. How has his journey changed him, and what wisdom will he share with his people?

As he reached his village with the sacred totem held high, he was ready to embrace his role as a guardian of his tribe's heritage and a keeper of the spirit of the sacred totem.

In essence, the main character should first be described.

1. Where do they live? What is their personality like?

2. The secondary characters should be shown. How do all these characters interact with each other?

3. The adventure should be introduced in their dialogue. What kind of magic does the quest contain?

4. As the journey begins, the challenges need to be stated, followed by how the main character overcomes them.

5. The story should conclude with a reflection on the main character. What did they learn from the adventure?

Chapter 9: Fireside Fables: Tales of Belonging

In the olden days, during seasons with long nights, under flickering lights or dancing flames, the natives would gather and share stories. But these weren't ordinary stories; they were fables and tales that have been passed down from generation to generation. These tales are usually full of adventures, wisdom, and a powerful feeling of belonging.

Fables aren't just for entertainment. They speak of things that concern us as humans and our surroundings. They

Fables shed light on matters that are close to the heart – things like the search for a place to fit in and the courage it takes to be one's self. [48]

shed light on matters close to the heart – things like the search for a place to fit in, the courage it takes to be one's self, and the importance of family and friends. These stories reveal how we are all connected to something bigger than ourselves. They teach us to appreciate Mother Earth even further.

Through these tales, the profound connection Native American cultures hold with their communities is uncovered, as well as the intricate dance of forging identity and the enduring spirit that seeks to find its rightful place within the grand threads of existence. The unwavering strength of legendary heroes and the whispers of ancestral spirits who guide us all on this timeless quest are highly spoken of. As we immerse ourselves in these stories, we are bound to get a deeper understanding of ourselves and the inherent human need for connection, and when the final word is spoken, it never fails to leave a lasting resonance within us long after the story is told.

This last chapter includes more fables and tales that reflect the search for identity, belonging, and community. Are you up for a few more stories? Well, you won't be disappointed. The tales of Awena, The Healer, and the Legend of Chief Seattle are laid out here for you.

You're on the last lap – keep reading, champ!

Awena the Healer

Once upon a time, in the Navajo land, there lived a curious girl named Awena. After the death of her mother, Awena struggled to find her place in her tribe. She knew she had the potential to do great things, but discovering what they were was difficult. Finally, she decided to go in search of the legendary Spider Woman. She had been told of the legend as a child and believed the being could help her.

Awena climbed a sacred mountain to find her purpose, her heart pounding with anticipation. [48]

One night, under the desert stars, Awena climbed a sacred mountain to find her purpose, her heart pounding with anticipation. At the top, she met an old woman, her skin etched with time and her eyes full of wisdom. It was the Spider Woman. She looked at the young girl and could sense why she came. "Child," Spider Woman said, her voice as gentle as a breeze. "You seek your purpose, but it lies within." Awena's heart hammered in her chest. "Your purpose lies not in what you chase, but in the gifts you already hold," the old woman continued, "you have a keen eye for herbs, a gentle touch with the sick, and a spirit that resonates with the Earth. Your purpose, child, is to be a healer, a bridge between your tribe and the land."

A wave of clarity washed over Awena. The visions and encounters that had been plaguing her – they weren't random. They were a reflection of her true self, leading her toward her destiny.

The legend took the girl in and began to groom her. She told Awena that everyone and everything is like a thread in a giant web. Awena listened, her heart swelling. She learned that every choice and every action rippled through the web. Kindness mended frayed strands while greed unraveled them. The land, the animals, the people – they were kin, bound by invisible threads.

Awena learned that patience was an important virtue to possess. Spider Woman showed her how to mend broken threads and how to honor the delicate balance. As days turned into weeks, Spider-Woman taught Awena the ways of a healer. She taught the young woman to be courageous, compassionate, and resilient. And so, Awena discovered her purpose: to be a healer.

She returned to the tribe, no longer a lost girl but a woman with a purpose. Her touch soothed wounds, and her knowledge of herbs brought comfort. She was told of a man sick to death, and she decided to pay him a visit.

Awena healing old man Herrick. "

Old man Herrick, a respected elder, lay shivering with a fever, his coughs echoing through the longhouse. Awena clutched her pouch of herbs, each one gathered under the watchful eye of Spider Woman. She placed a cool hand on his forehead. Closing her eyes, Awena whispered a prayer to Spider Woman, the creator. Memories of her lessons flooded back – the soothing touch of yucca root and the calming scent of lavender, and she got to work.

By morning, the fever had broken. A weak smile graced Herrick's lips as he looked at Awena: "You are a weaver, too, child," he rasped, "weaving health back into tired bodies." Awena's heart swelled. She wasn't just a healer – just like Spider-Woman, she was mending the tears in the web of life one person at a time.

The Legend of Chief Seattle

In the land of Native American tribes, Suquamish and Duwamish, a great leader was born. His name was Chief Seattle. Chief Seattle, or as he was sometimes called, Sealth, was a well-known and respected leader.

From his youth, whispers of the spirit world snaked through the rustling leaves and gurgling streams, forming a deep connection within him – to the land and his people. He listened to all the tales told by his elders, sagas of warriors and of spirits dwelling in every mountain peak and rushing waterway.

As years passed by for the legend, Chief Seattle walked the ancestral paths, absorbing the sacred rituals and traditions that were the lifeblood of his tribe. He

Chief Seattle, or as he was sometimes called, Sealth."

honored the spirits that laid beneath the Earth, leaving offerings of fragrant tobacco and sweetgrass as a humble thank you for the bounty that sustained them.

But, Chief Seattle's vision stretched beyond the borders of his own tribe. He understood the unifying melody that bound all Native American hearts. He tirelessly stitched alliances and treaties, a bulwark against the people who sought to sever their connection to their ancestral lands.

One day, he gathered his people beneath a colossal cedar; its ancient boughs a protective canopy. As sunlight filtered through, dappling the faces of his tribe, Chief Seattle spoke. His voice was a deep rumble. He spoke of how all living things were connected and of the Earth as a sacred gift entrusted to them by the Great Spirit.

"Our ancestors walk beside us," he declared, his gaze sweeping across the rapt faces. "Their spirits are in the wind, guiding our every step. We honor them by treading lightly upon Mother Nature, making sure the delicate balance remains unbroken."

His words struck a chord within them, igniting a fierce sense of belonging and purpose. They understood – their identity was as inseparable from the land as the bark from the towering trees, and their traditions were woven into the very fabric of the natural world.

Under Chief Seattle's unwavering leadership, the tribe embraced their sacred duty as guardians of the Earth. With unwavering resolve, they protected the verdant forests and life-giving rivers that cradled their existence. They found strength in their shared heritage, drawing upon the wisdom of their ancestors to navigate the treacherous currents of a changing world.

Governor of Washington, Isaac Stevens, negotiated with Chief Seattle to sell the land, which is now the city of Seattle. "

Sometime in 1854, when the territorial Governor of Washington, Isaac Stevens, visited their land, he negotiated with Chief Seattle for the sale of the land, which is now the city of Seattle. It was named in honor of the Chief. In response to the Governor, Chief Seattle gave his famous speech:

"How can you buy or sell the sky? The land? The idea is strange to us. If we do not own the freshness of the air and the sparkle of the water, how can you buy them? Every part of this earth is sacred to my people. Every shining pine needle, every sandy shore, every mist in the dark woods, every meadow, every humming insect. All are holy in the memory and experience of my people...

If we sell you our land, remember that the air is precious to us, that the air shares its spirit with all the life it supports. The wind that gave our grandfather his first breath also received his last sigh. The wind also gives our children the spirit of life. So, if we sell you our land, you must keep it apart and sacred, a place where man can go to taste the wind that is sweetened by the meadow flowers. Will you teach your children what we have taught our children? That the earth is our mother? What befalls the earth befalls all the sons of the earth.

This we know: the earth does not belong to man; man belongs to the earth. All things are connected like the blood that unites us all. Man did not weave the web of life; he is merely a strand in it. Whatever he does to the web, he does to himself. One thing we know: Our God is also your God. The earth is precious to Him and to harm the earth is to heap contempt on its Creator."

(Earth in Balance: Ecology and the Human Spirit, Gore 1992, 159)

A hush fell over the gathering as Chief Seattle's words hung heavy in the air. Some faces creased further in solemn reflection. The weight of his message settled deep within them – a truth resonating with the very core of their being. After all, their people had always lived in harmony with the land.

Chief Seattle's voice was a powerful echo of their own connection to the Earth. His words, carried on the wind, ignited a fire in the hearts of his people. This wasn't just a speech; it was a passionate plea to honor the land that sustained them.

The impact of his words reverberated far beyond that day. They became a timeless message – a beacon for generations to come. Chief Seattle's voice became a rallying cry for those who championed the environment – a powerful reminder of our responsibility to protect the Earth. His legacy continues to inspire countless individuals and movements – their voices rising in unison for the land and the rights of those who have always called it home.

Activity: End-of-Book Quiz

Instructions:

Choose the correct answer for each question. Feel free to refer back to the book for help. Once you've answered all the questions, check your answers to see how well you remember the inspiring stories of Native American culture and folklore.

Chapter 1

Who were the two powerful beings that were referred to as the cosmic mother and father?

a. Sun and Moon

b. Spider Woman and Tawa, the sun god

c. Eagle and Bear

d. Buffalo and Deer

Why did the Wampanoag people respect nature so much?

_____

_____

_____

Chapter 2

Who was a famous Native American leader known for his role in the Battle of Little Bighorn?

a. Chief Sitting Bull

b. Chief Seattle

c. Sacagawea

d. Geronimo

Chapter 3

What lessons did you learn from the tales about the stars?

_____

_____

_____

Chapter 4

Why was the buffalo important to many Native American tribes?

    a. It provided food, clothing, and shelter.

    b. It was a symbol of fear and danger.

    c. It was believed to possess magical powers.

    d. It was considered sacred and worshiped.

What is the symbolism of the buffalo's life cycle to the people of the Plains tribes?

    a. Laughter and child-bearing.

    b. Unity and abundance.

    c. Sacrifice and wisdom.

    d. Flowing rivers and green gardens.

Chapter 5

What is a prophecy?

    a. A historical event.

    b. A prediction of the future.

    c. A religious ceremony.

    d. A moral lesson.

Which Native American tribe is particularly associated with the prophecy of the Seventh Generation?

    a. Cherokee

    b. Iroquois

    c. Navajo

    d. Apache

Chapter 6

Why did the god of summer decide to help Glooscap and the Mi'kmaq people?

    a. Glooscap was strong and mighty.

    b. Glooscap sang him songs of praise.

    c. Glooscap offered prayers and sacrifices.

    d. Glooscap came to him in humility.

Chapter 7

Which two of these are famous trickster figures in Native American mythology known for their mischievous antics?

    a. Raven

    b. Coyote

    c. Bear

    d. Fox

What lesson do trickster tales often teach us?

    a. The importance of honesty and integrity.

    b. The consequences of greed and selfishness.

    c. The value of hard work and perseverance.

    d. The dangers of trusting strangers.

Chapter 8

What role do the winds play in many Native American stories?

    a. They carry messages from the spirits.

    b. They bring storms and disasters.

    c. They guide travelers on their journeys.

    d. They whisper secrets to those who listen.

What is a vision quest?

    a. A journey to find lost treasure.

    b. A quest for knowledge and understanding.

    c. A search for a missing person.

    d. A battle against supernatural forces.

Chapter 9

What lesson does the story of Chief Seattle teach us about belonging?

a. The importance of preserving cultural heritage.

b. The value of environmental stewardship.

c. The need for unity and cooperation.

d. All of the above.

Answer Key

Chapter 2

Test of Knowledge Answers:

1. Sitting Bull was named Jumping Badger after his birth. He earned the name Sitting Bull after striking one of the enemy warriors with a coup stick at 14.

2. General George Custer.

3. General Alfred Sully.

4. Tahlequah, Oklahoma.

5. Due to new laws that allowed the relocation of aboriginal tribes, promising them better opportunities in big cities.

6. Mankiller returned to her Cherokee home in Oklahoma by 1977.

Chapter 3

Shooting for the Stars Quiz Answers:

1. A
2. D
3. B
4. A
5. C
6. B
7. D

8. A
9. B
10. A

Chapter 4

True or False Answers:

1. False
2. True
3. True
4. False
5. False
6. True
7. False
8. True

Chapter 7

Two truths and a Lie Answers:

1. Foxes
2. Vultures
3. He wanted the rattlesnake's head
4. To know that vanity is a folly
5. His wisdom
6. True beauty lies in the adornments we wear
7. Failed to realize his folly

End of Book Quiz Answers:

Questions from Chapter 1:

1. B.
2. They understood that nature is part of the Circle of Life.

Questions from Chapter 2:

1. A.

Questions from Chapter 3:

1. A.

Questions from Chapter 4:
1. C.
2. A.

Questions from Chapter 5:
1. B.
2. D.

Questions from Chapter 6:
1. D.

Questions from Chapter 7:
1. A and B.
2. A, B, and D.

Questions from Chapter 8:
1. A.
2. B

Questions from Chapter 9:
1. B

Conclusion

You've now reached the end of this exciting journey through Native American tales. Some of the stories you read spoke about people who lived long ago, settling down and growing crops or wandering around hunting and foraging for food and other necessities. They spoke different languages, had a colorful culture, and passed down many legends. From their tales, you learned how the Native Americans explained how the world came to be and which heroes they believed played a part in their early history.

You also read about some of the bravest acts of Native American heroes throughout history and where they found the courage to triumph when everything seemed lost. As you've learned, having a leader was just as important to Native tribes as it is and has been in every other world culture.

Besides its role in creation, the natural world (especially the sky and the earth) was also considered a powerful source of blessings. Native Americans have many tales about the stars, retelling how these shiny objects guided them through adventures.

Hunters, warriors, and farmers alike lived in close communities, and to form these communities, they took inspiration from nature. One of the main characters in forming their peaceful communities was the buffalo. This powerful animal was both a gift and a source of many lessons that were passed down through generations.

Native Americans always had unique ways of celebrating nature. They believed that, like the buffalo, many other creatures brought people gifts, blessings, and lessons. They taught people how to live together with nature and all the natural beings around them because they could all help each other out.

However, as you've learned, the Native tribes also knew how tricky some creatures could be. While the stories about cunning tricksters can also teach one to respect nature, they also show that sometimes you must be very careful about how you approach people.

Nature holds many mysteries, too, according to Native American tales. Some of these mysteries invite people to unforgettable adventures, while others can show a person how brave they can be when encountering an unexpected challenge.

Like everyone else in this world, the ancient tribes knew how important it was for a person to find a place where they could be happy. Their fables speak about young people embarking on the journey of learning to be the best versions of themselves while respecting their link to nature and other people.

Many of the lessons from these Native American tales can be applied today. People today can build relationships with nature and each other just as closely as their Native ancestors were taught to do. Whether it's your neighbors, friends, classmates, family members, teachers, pets, or your favorite place outdoors, there is always a way to form a connection with your surroundings. You just have to find the inspiration to reach out, and this book has given you a treasure trove of information on how to do that.

Part 2: Empowering Native American Stories For Children

Embarking on Empowering Journeys of Resilience, Wisdom, and Cultural Pride to Enrich Young Hearts and Minds

Introduction

It's common to talk about Native Americans as if they're all the same, no matter where they're from. However, every tribe has its own unique identity, with a rich history, culture, traditions, beliefs, and legends. There are many interesting tales and facts about each Native American tribe that show their similarities and their differences. This book is a great way for kids to learn about how they lived through a collection of stories and myths. Pictures and maps help you get a better idea of the information provided, and the topics are presented in a way that makes them easy to understand.

There is a lot that you can learn from the Native Americans. Still, many schools from other cultures mostly focus on history from a European point of view. They talk about the wars and only touch on the horrible treatment given to the tribes during the relocation to reservations. Yet there is so much more to them than their conflict with the colonists and settlers. Every tribe has a way of life that developed long before anyone sailed across the ocean and set foot on their shores. The culture of every tribe is unique, and they can give you a new way of looking at the world.

While this book is meant to be educational, it's not some boring textbook. There are snippets of information to help you understand the basics of each tribe. Then, it dives into stories that go deeper into the experiences of people who lived through the days when the continent was just for them. These tales are fun and exciting, and they'll make you think about using their lessons in your life. If you enjoy learning new things, this book will give you plenty of stories and facts you've never heard!

Chapter 1: The Navajo Way

The Navajo are a major Native American tribe from the Southwestern United States. They have the biggest reservation in the country, which stretches across the Four Corners. This region includes the states of Utah, Arizona, New Mexico, and Colorado. The Navajo people have a rich storytelling tradition, passing down tales of their tribe's mythology from generation to generation. Their artwork also tells stories, using pictures and symbols to represent major figures or events from their history and religion.

Flag of the Navajo Nation[47]

Hogans

Hogans are the type of home that the Navajo people live in. They can be built in shapes like cones, squares, rounded tops, or have multiple sides. The walls are made from packed earth, stone, and timber, while the roofs are created using tree bark. By packing mud onto the walls of their hogans, the Navajo were able to insulate and protect their homes from the summer heat, and it also kept their hogans warm in the cold winter months. Many Navajo still live in hogans, as these dwellings are considered very energy efficient, making it easy to stay comfortable without needing things like air conditioners or heaters.

Navajo Winter Hogan.[48]

Important Symbols of the Navajo Tribe

Sun: This symbol represents everything in the universe being in harmony. All living things need the sun to survive, and all living things are at their best when they work together. The sun also brings good luck, happiness, and plentiful harvests.

Water: This symbol represents life and balance. Like the sun, all living things need water to survive, but while the sun brings life from the outside, water gives life from the inside. It also shows how nothing is permanent. Just like how the course of a river can change over time, life also continues to change.

Lightning: This symbol represents speed and agility. Lightning streaks all across the sky in a single instant, often moving faster than sound. It can also be a warning against doing things that could bring bad luck.

Bear: This symbol represents strength, endurance, and durability. The bear is a very powerful animal, being large and imposing. When you see a bear, it is a sign to accept your past in order to overcome obstacles and have a successful future. It is also a warning to prepare and build up defenses against danger.

Thunderbird: This symbol represents a sudden rush of happiness. As a mythological creature, the thunderbird is believed to only appear when the blessings given to the tribe are plentiful. It can also be seen as a sign of peace and serenity for those who see the great creature.

Arrow: This symbol represents protection and safety. Bows and arrows were one of the main weapons used by the Navajo people to hunt and fight, so the arrow is considered something that helps to keep them safe from predators and enemies. It also serves as a warning to anyone who might seek to harm them that they are willing to use violence to protect themselves and their people.

The Coyote

The Coyote is a trickster god in Navajo mythology with power over the rain. He is an important figure in many of the stories the Navajo people tell, always creating mischief and causing problems for those he meets. The Coyote won his wife, Changing Bear, by cheating in a contest and using his magic to make her evil. Like the Coyote, Changing Bear was able to transform from a human into an animal form. Together, they became a dangerous couple, always looking for new ways to cause trouble. Nobody knows why the Coyote enjoys being nasty and tricking people like that. Still, whenever he turns up, anyone he meets must be careful not to become his next victim.

Changing Bear and Her Brothers

After the Coyote taught Changing Bear how to use the innate power of water to find out the location of her brothers, she turned into a human and went to meet them. She flattered them by complimenting their hair and reminded them how she used to comb it for them to check for lice.

The brothers of Changing Bear didn't want their hair to become filled with lice, so they agreed to let her comb it for them like she did before the Coyote made her evil. They trusted their sister and turned their backs on her. She transformed into a she-bear, mauling them to death while the Coyote howled in laughter.

The Coyote and the Giant

Sometimes, the Coyote's mischief can be helpful, even though that's not his intention.

There was a giant who was terrorizing the land, destroying villages, and eating the people he found there, including their small children. One day, the Coyote raced past the giant, and the giant ran after him. However, the giant was too slow and couldn't catch up. The Coyote returned to the giant and convinced the monster that he could make it so the giant could run as fast as him. The giant agreed, and the Coyote broke his leg and then spit on it, telling the giant that this would heal it and strengthen the bones and muscles. This turned out to be a trick, and the giant now had trouble walking, unable to catch up to the smallest of children as they ran away from him!

The Yéii

The Yéii are benevolent or good divine spirits that help the Navajo people. While there are many different types of Yéii, the ones most honored are the Holy People (Diyin Diné'e). They are connected to the forces of nature and were among the first beings who eventually helped create our world. The Yéii have power over things like rain, wind, earth, plants, and fire. When the time came to settle down, they shaped the world around them, creating things in nature that let people survive. It's considered a good idea to offer thanks and blessings to the Yéii, as they can use their powers to help bring good fortune to the Navajo people.

Diné Bahane' (Story of the People)

The Diné Bahane' is the Navajo people's story about the creation of the universe. It tells the tale of how there were originally four worlds, each bringing something different into being. The fourth and final world was the one where regular humans came from. There were also the Yéii, divine spirits known as the Holy People, who helped to shape the world as it's known today. The First Man and First Woman journeyed across the four worlds to explore the creatures and environments that came into existence.

The Dark World (First World)

In the beginning, the Dark World (Ni' Hodiłhił) was a chaotic and unruly place. The four seas stretched as far as the eye could see, and floating at their center was a small island. Many beings lived in the Dark World. The first and foremost were the Diyin Dine'é, also known as the Holy People. They were powerful supernatural spirits who used their magic to shape the land and bring knowledge to others. Also living in the Dark World were the Coyote, the Four Rulers of the Seas, Beings of the Mists, the Insect People, and the Bat People. The Bat People were considered Air-Spirit People, using their massive wings to control the skies.

When the First Man and the First Woman came into being, they lived on separate ends of the island. Both of them built large fires to help them stay warm at night. Upon seeing each other's fires from across the island, they set out to find whoever had made the fire. After walking for days, the First Man and Woman met at the island's center and realized they were meant to be together. They fell in love, deciding to live as husband and wife. The pair were happy to have found one another and for a while, everything seemed to be perfect. They used great power to create the Holy People, who banded together to form the First Tribe.

However, their happiness would not last, as the Dark World was a violent place. All the different beings were constantly at war with one another, but the First Man and Woman wanted to live in peace. They were able to get wings from the Air-Spirit People, which allowed them and their tribe to explore far across the seas in the hope that they could find a new land where they would be able to live in harmony with everything around them. After searching for days, they failed to find any new lands but instead discovered an opening in the sky that was a great distance away in the East. The tribe flew through the opening, chancing that whatever they may find would be better than the Dark World.

The Blue World (Second World)

After flying through the opening in the East of the Dark World, the First Man and Woman led their tribe as they entered the Blue World (Ni' Hodootł'izh). They found that nearly all the creatures living there were colored blue. There were blue-feathered birds and blue-furred animals, and the blue swallows were the main inhabitants of the Blue World. The blue swallows' ruler, Chief Swallow, was offended when he saw the Holy People enter his domain from the Dark World. He confronted them and demanded that they leave at once.

Although the First Man and Woman liked the Blue World, they knew they couldn't stay. The Swallow Chief threatened to attack the pair, and they didn't want to fight. The First Man uncovered a deposit of beautiful black gemstones known as jet, and he used these gemstones with wood from the trees of the Blue World to create a magical wand. With his new wand, the First Man made a wish that their tribe could walk into the sky, where there was another opening far to the South. They left the Blue World together, leaving the Chief Swallow and the other creatures behind, hoping the next place they found could be their new home.

The Yellow World (Third World)

When the Holy People emerged from the opening, they saw they were in the Yellow World (Ni' Hałtsooí). It was a wondrous place, with rushing rivers and towering mountains dominating the landscape. Like the other worlds, the Yellow World was filled with many strange and interesting creatures, yet there was no sun in the sky, so everything was covered in darkness. The Holy People followed the rivers and stopped at the spot where two rivers came together to form a cross. Behind them, the Sacred Mountains stretched so high the tribe couldn't even see their peaks. It seemed like a good place to live, as the creatures weren't at war and didn't try to drive them out.

Unfortunately, the Coyote from the Dark World had followed the Holy People, looking for new ways to create mischief. There was a monster in the Yellow World known as Tééhoołtsódii, or the Big Water Creature. The Coyote stole her children, and in her anger, she unleashed a great flood. Since the Holy People lived at the point where the rivers converged, the great flood came and washed away their settlement. Everything they had built was destroyed. Knowing they couldn't stay in the Yellow World any longer, the First Man and Woman searched the lands until they found an opening in the West. They took their tribe and left through an opening, uncertain if fate would be kinder in the next world.

The White World (Fourth World)

The Holy People traveled through the opening and came out the other side into the White World (Ni' Hodisxǫs). In this world, the magic of the Holy People was even more powerful than before. They built a new settlement on the banks of a great river but were careful not to place their homes too close to the water. The First Man had taken some soil from the Yellow World, and with his wand, he used it to recreate the Sacred Mountains in the White World. The Holy People then created the Sun, Moon, Stars, and even the Seasons.

The Coyote followed the Holy People again and went to the tribe's settlement to create more mischief. He threw a stone in the river and declared that if the stone sank, anyone who died would be sent back to the previous worlds. As soon as the stone hit the water, it dropped to the bottom of the river, and the Coyote told the Holy People that he had created Death. This upset the tribe, but there were no more worlds where they could go, so they had no choice but to accept that Death was now a part of their reality.

The First Man and Woman gave birth to a child named the White Shell Woman (Yoołgaii Asdzą́ą́). When she grew up, she became known as the Changing Woman (Asdzą́ą́ Nádleehé), and fell in love with the Sun. The Changing Woman gave birth to the Hero Twins, a pair of beings named Monster Slayer (Naayéé' Neizghání) and Born For Water (Tóbájíshchíní). The Hero Twins went on many adventures across the White World, where they encountered the Anaye, a group of evil monsters that lived in the dark places untouched by their father, the Sun. The Hero Twins spent many Seasons battling the monsters, eventually ridding the world of the Anaye.

After coming to the White World, the Holy People had children who were all human beings. Unlike their parents, the humans had no powers but were inventive and had strong inner spirits. They created tools, weapons, and new shelters that kept them safe from the outside world. The humans explored the lands and came together to form new tribes. However, they never forgot where they came from and honored their ancestors through sacred rituals and ceremonies. The modern tribes still practice many of these rituals and ceremonies, keeping the spirit of the Holy People alive.

Chapter Round-Up Activity

Can you tell what someone is trying to tell you when they only use a simple picture to communicate? The Navajo have many symbols that help them express different ideas about the world around them. See if you can match these symbols to their meanings:

Bear

Peace and Serenity

Sun

Ruler of the Blue World

Water

Good Luck and Happiness

Lightning

Trickster God

Thunderbird

Evil Monster

Wand

Safety and Protection

Strength, Endurance, and
Durability

Anaye

Speed and Agility

Chief Swallow

Made With Jet

Arrow

Life and Balance

Coyote

Chapter 2: Lakota Legends: The Buffalo and the Sioux

The Lakota tribe are members of the Sioux Nation. They are one of the three main tribes that make up the Sioux. Nowadays, they mostly live in North and South Dakota. However, the Sioux were originally spread across much of the Midwest of the United States, including the Great Plains region. Like all members of the Sioux Nation, the Lakota speak the Siouan language, but their dialect is known as Lakȟótiyapi. Around 1730, the Cheyenne people introduced the Lakota to horses, which became a major part of the Sioux culture.

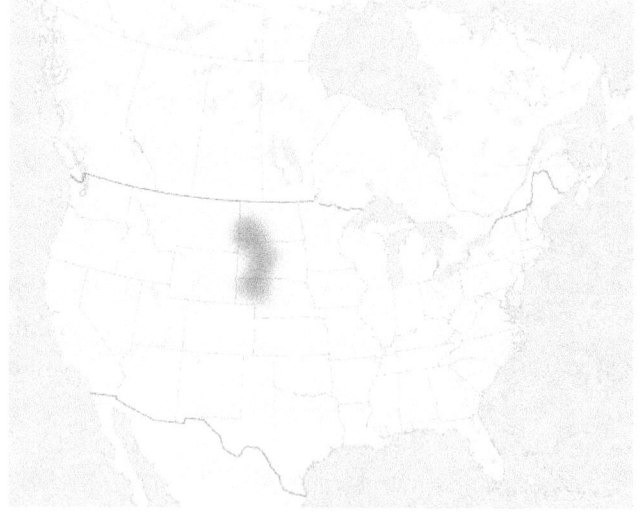

The Map of Lakota.[49]

Lakota Subtribes

There are seven subtribes of the Lakota. Their names are in the Lakota language, but they have English translations that many non-Native Americans know them by. The seven subtribes of the Lakota include:

Blackfoot/Blackfeet (Sihásapa): The Blackfoot subtribe of the Lakota has a name similar to the Blackfoot Confederacy, which lives in the Great Plains part of the United States. Still, they are entirely separate from one another. The Lakota Blackfeet dwelled in the western portion of North and South Dakota, but they now live on the Standing Rock Reservation, which stretches across both North and South Dakota, and the Cheyenne River Reservation in South Dakota, where they share the land with other subtribes of the Lakota.

Brulé/Burnt Thighs (Sičháŋǧu): They mainly lived on the Rosebud Indian Reservation in the southwestern portion of South Dakota, but smaller groups of the Brulé subtribe have settled on the Lower Brule Indian Reservation in central South Dakota along the western bank of the Missouri River. There are also some members of the Brulé on the Pine Ridge Indian Reservation, located to the west of the Rosebud Indian Reservation. Bob Barker, the former longtime host of the CBS game show *The Price Is Right*, was a member of the Brulé, and spent much of his youth on the Rosebud Indian Reservation.

Miniconjou/Plants by the Water (Mnikȟówožu): They once lived in the western portion of South Dakota, from the Black Hills to the Platte River. Currently, they inhabit the west-central part of the state. They were called "Plants by the Water" because the Miniconjou built settlements near rivers and grew their crops nearby. The Two Kettles subtribe was originally part of the Miniconjou but split off in 1840 to form their own subtribe. The Miniconjou's most famous chief was Touch the Clouds, who was revered as a great warrior and diplomat.

Sans Arc/Without Bows (Itázipčho): While their name "Sans Arc" is French for "Without Bows," their true name means "no markings." Their name refers to the fact that the Sans Arc hunters never put markings on their arrows. Most tribes would mark their arrows to prove who killed the prey they hunted, especially buffalo or bison. However, the Sans Arc people left their arrows unmarked so that everyone could share the meat they received from their kills. This generosity was well-known within the Lakota tribe, and the tale of the White Buffalo Woman claimed it was due to this trait that she gave the peace pipe to the Sans Arc people.

Hunkpapa/Head of the Circle (Húŋkpapȟa): Along with several other Lakota subtribes, they were among the first Native American tribes to fight alongside the United States during the American Indian Wars. The Hunkpapa got their name because they built their lodges at the entrance to the Great Council circle, where all the members of the Sioux Nation would meet. Sitting Bull, a famous Lakota leader who fought in the Battle of Little Bighorn against the United States Army's 7th Cavalry Regiment under the command of Lieutenant Colonel George Armstrong Custer, was a member of the Hunkpapa.

Two Kettles/Two Boilings (Oóhenuŋpa): They are considered members of the Central Lakota and currently live on the Cheyenne River Indian Reservation. During the 19th century, they lived in smaller groups along the Missouri and Cheyenne Rivers, migrating with the herds of buffalo or bison. The Two Kettles people had a mostly peaceful relationship with the European settlers, engaging in trade and welcoming them as guests. Unlike some other subtribes of the Lakota, they were willing to sign peace treaties, promising not to attack the settlers unless it was in self-defense.

Oglala/They Scatter Their Own (Oglála): They began trading beaver and bison furs with the European settlers who came out west during the early 19th century. However, tensions between the settlers and Native Americans increased – especially after the Sioux signed the Fort Laramie Treaty with the United States federal government in 1868. After that, the Oglala resisted any attempt to force them onto a reservation. Ultimately, they had no choice but to submit; they now live on the Pine Ridge Indian Reservation in South Dakota. Crazy Horse was a leader of the Oglala and a hero to his people for his actions during the Battle of Little Bighorn.

The Chief and the Buffalo

The flickering flame from a single candle cast a soft orange light over a piece of paper lying on the small table. The Lakota Chief sat beside the table and stared at the treaty he was supposed to sign . . . to agree with his tribe moving from their ancestral lands to a reservation. The man from the government promised the Chief that they would be very comfortable and have the entire reservation to themselves, allowing them to do whatever they wanted within its borders. But White Men had promised his people many things over the years, and those promises were rarely kept.

Chief Sitting Bull.[60]

As the hours ticked away, the Chief remained undecided about signing the treaty. Most of the neighboring tribes had already left for the reservations, and his tribe was far too small to put up a fight by themselves. If they tried, they would be killed for certain. Yet the idea of dooming his people to live in what was basically an outdoor prison didn't seem like a much better fate. He was frustrated that he was being forced to choose between two terrible options. Should he sign his name on the treaty, he would forever be remembered as the chief who surrendered.

Glancing out the opening of his teepee, the Chief saw that the moon was full, and the stars were shining brightly, blanketing the lands in a silvery glow. A cool breeze was drifting through the air, fighting off the overbearing summer heat. He decided to go for a walk to clear his head since he wasn't making any progress, just sitting there in his home. Emerging from his teepee, the Chief strolled through his village, wondering how his people would see him if he agreed to the treaty's terms. Would they spit at him, calling him a coward and a traitor? What if he refused to sign it? Would they use their final breath to curse his name as they died for a lost cause? It was an impossible situation.

When the Chief reached the edge of the village, he greeted the tribesman standing guard. There was no sign of trouble beyond the village, so the Chief headed off into the plains alone and unarmed. He walked for a long while before reaching the river bank, and he wanted to dip his toes in the water while having a quick rest. The Chief sat on the river's edge, letting the rushing river wash over his sore feet, still thinking about his big decision. The sound of footsteps behind him caused him to leap up and whirl around. Even though he wasn't carrying a weapon, he was ready to fight to the death with his hands.

"Do not be alarmed," a voice said.

The Chief wasn't alarmed anymore – now he was in awe. The Great White Buffalo stood before him, towering over the Chief and staring down at him with two huge black eyes. When the Buffalo spoke, his mouth didn't move, and no sounds came from him. Instead, the Chief heard the Buffalo's voice speaking within his mind.

"I know who you are, and I am not scared," he told the Buffalo. "But my heart is heavy tonight. I must make a big decision, and I do not know what to do."

"You wear your burdens like a cloak, Little Chief. I can tell your soul is troubled. I understand why you struggle to make your decision. You feel there is little difference between confinement on a reservation and certain death in a fight."

"That is true, oh Great One," the Chief replied. "Please, tell me which I should choose."

"I cannot tell you that," the Buffalo said. "This is something you must decide for yourself. Look deep in your heart and listen to what it tells you."

"My heart was broken long ago, when my people were scattered and forced to survive apart from one another. It has been silent for many years."

"Your heart is like your people," the Buffalo stated. "It may be in many different pieces, but those pieces can still be put back together and become stronger than ever before."

The Chief closed his eyes and looked inward. He told the Buffalo, "I know if I do not sign the treaty, our enemy will come to wipe us out. Many would say it is better to die a warrior's death than surrendering to live a coward's life."

"Yes, many would say that," the Buffalo agreed. "But what do you say, Little Chief?"

"I do not want to watch my people die," the Chief admitted. "I also do not want to watch them die on the inside because we are stuck on a reservation, unable to live free in the way we have always lived."

"There would be many changes for your people living on a reservation. They would have to change, too."

"We do not want to change!" the Chief cried. "I do not want to change! My people have lived a certain way since before my great-great-grandfather was chief. If we are forced to change, we would no longer be Lakota. Maybe it would be better to fight and die. At least we would fight and die as who we are now."

"Everything changes, Little Chief," the Buffalo said calmly. "Look at the children of your tribe – do they not grow older and change? What about the flowers and trees? They change with the seasons, blooming and dying and being reborn. The weather is always changing – sometimes the sun shines, and sometimes the thunderstorms bring rain. The moon changes shape, and the stars change their positions in the sky. Day changes into night, and night into day."

"I understand what you mean, but this is not the same," the Chief insisted. "When the trees go bare in the winter, their leaves return in the spring. The sun disappears when it is the moon's turn to rule the skies, but it always returns at dawn. If my people change, we will change for good. We will become like the White Man and lose everything that makes us Lakota."

"Do you think death would be better than that?" the Buffalo asked.

The Chief shook his head, but there was anger in his voice when he said, "No, death would not be better. But how can I live knowing I am responsible for taking the spirit of my people away?"

"Just because you will change does not mean you will lose everything that makes your people Lakota. You can keep the spirit alive as long as your people still live. You can keep many parts of your culture and pass your memories down to your children. Show them what it means to be Lakota. Share your stories and teach them your rituals. If you do not let that spirit die, no matter what else changes, you will always be Lakota."

"We will always be Lakota," the Chief echoed, thinking deeply about the Great White Buffalo's words.

"I think you know what choice you will make now," the Buffalo said. "I have watched over your people since the beginning. And I will continue watching over them long after you are gone. Rest easy tonight, Little Chief. Everything will be right when the sun rises again."

The Chief opened his eyes and sat up with a jolt. He looked around, realizing he was back in his teepee. The candle on the table had burned out, but the treaty remained exactly where he'd left it. There was sunlight streaming through the opening of his teepee, and he wondered if his encounter with the Great White Buffalo had all been a dream. However, when he went outside to stretch his legs, the tribesman who stood guard the night before rushed over to him.

"Chief! I was about to gather a search party to go find you," the tribesman told him. "I never saw you return last night."

"Everything is fine. There is no need to worry," the Chief assured him. "I have made my decision about the treaty. I will sign it, and we will leave these lands for the last time. But no matter what changes, we will keep the spirit of our tribe alive in our hearts and minds. We will forever be Lakota."

Kohana's First Buffalo Hunt

Kohana gripped his bow tightly and made sure his arrows were within reach in his quiver. His horse neighed and shook its head, mirroring his own anxiousness. This was going to be his first buffalo hunt. After today, he would be seen as a man. However, while he had no trouble hitting the targets when practicing with his bow, a charging buffalo would not be as easy. The hunters hadn't even started riding, yet his heart was already beating as fast as the drums during the previous night's ceremony.

"Try to remain calm," said Akecheta.

He was their tribe's best hunter. Akecheta killed his first buffalo when he was only ten years old, and he'd been leading the buffalo hunts for the last five years. Kohana nodded and tried to do as the older man suggested, but it wasn't simple. The last of the hunters finally mounted their horses, and the party was ready to head off across the plains.

"Ride hard, aim true, and make the kills clean," Akecheta commanded. "Now we go!"

A dozen sets of hooves stomped against the ground and sounded like thunder. Kohana kicked at his horse and sent it galloping along with the rest of the group. He was a skilled rider, so he was able to keep up with the more seasoned hunters. They followed the tracks left by the buffalo and soon caught up with the herd. Seeing them up close as they stampeded with their powerful legs was very different from seeing one brought back following the hunt. Kohana's nerves were on edge, and he feared his hands would shake too much to make a good shot.

Akecheta brought his horse beside Kohana's and shouted, "Look for a straggler! Aim for the neck! You can do this!"

With the older man's encouragement, Kohana scanned the herd to find a buffalo lagging behind the others. The moment he spotted a smaller one struggling to stay with the pack, he turned his horse and took off. This was his chance to prove himself to the tribe. He reached for an arrow from his quiver and set it against his bowstring. Pulling the arrow back, he aimed carefully and released it. The arrow soared through the air and plunged into the side of the smaller buffalo's neck. It groaned loudly as it toppled to the ground, sliding a foot or two through the tall grass before stopping.

"Good shot, Kohana!" Akecheta exclaimed. "You got it!"

Kohana slowed his horse and rode around the slain buffalo to make sure it was dead. He got off his horse and kneeled beside the creature, placing his hand on top of its head. Closing his eyes, he offered a short blessing, saying, "May your spirit find peace with the ancestors and your body be a great boon to my people. I thank you for your sacrifice, so that my people may eat your meat, use your bones in our crafts, and use your hide to stay warm."

At the end of the hunt, the party returned to their village with three buffalo, including the one killed by Kohana. He was beaming a smile at his people as they congratulated him. Their chief emerged from his teepee and embraced Kohana.

"You have proven your skills as a hunter, young one," the chief said. "You are now a man."

Iktómi (The Spider)

Iktómi is a trickster spirit in Lakota culture who usually appears in the form of a spider. However, he has the ability to shapeshift into any form he wants. Sometimes, he shapeshifts into the form of a human and can be recognized by the red, white, and yellow paint he wears and the black rings he has around his eyes. Many of the stories involving Iktómi include morals and lessons to help guide the children of the tribe in behaving the right way. He is also credited as the creator of the first dreamcatcher, spinning his webs to make a net that prevents bad spirits from reaching the sleeping humans.

The Spider and the Oak Tree

Iktómi was sleeping on a web he'd spun between the branches of an old oak tree. He was dreaming a pleasant dream when his web suddenly shook violently. Waking up in a daze, he looked around to see what was causing everything to shake. When he glanced down toward the ground, he saw a young Lakota man hacking at the tree trunk with an axe.

"What do you think you are doing?" Iktómi cried. "You are destroying my home!"

The Lakota man looked up at him and replied, "Quiet! You are a spider and can spin your web anywhere. My people need the wood from this tree to feed our fires and carve our totem poles."

This made Iktómi angry, and he shouted back, "You are a man and can cut down any tree you want! Go cut down another tree and leave my home alone!"

"There are no trees bigger than this one anywhere around here," the man argued. "This was the one my chief told me to cut down. I must obey my chief, so you must find somewhere else to put your web."

Iktómi transformed into a field sparrow and flew away, cursing the Lakota man for stealing his home. He wanted revenge, and he knew exactly how to get it. Soaring over the plains, he searched the lands below for the instrument of his vengeance. As soon as he spotted it, he dived toward the ground. Just before he slammed into the earth, he stretched out his wings to halt his descent. At the last moment, he transformed into a black wolf and landed softly on his paws. The gray-furred leader of the buffalo wolf pack Iktómi was seeking came forward to confront him.

"Who are you, and what are you doing here?" the Wolf Chief asked, showing his fangs in a threatening manner.

"You know who I am," Iktómi said in the Wolf's language. "I helped your father escape a trap that the White Man hid near the river."

"You are Iktómi?" the Wolf questioned, suspicious of the newcomer. "Prove it."

"As you wish." The black wolf transformed into a spider right before the other's eyes. Iktómi then turned back into a wolf. "Satisfied?"

"Very well. I believe you now, Iktómi," said the Wolf Chief. "Why have you come to my pack?"

Iktómi grinned, showing rows of razor-sharp teeth. "The Lakota who live just over those hills have been planning a hunt. They want wolf fur to decorate their teepees and keep them warm when the winter comes. I heard them say they will come for you at dawn tomorrow. But if you strike first..."

"They will never see it coming." the Wolf said, finishing the spider's sentence. "Thank you, Iktómi, for giving us this warning. We will not waste it."

Iktómi transformed into a swallow again and flew away, congratulating himself on his clever plan. The wolves would attack the Lakota village in the night, and those responsible for cutting down his tree would surely be killed. He traveled across the plains until he reached the village, perching atop the largest teepee. It belonged to the Lakota chief, the man who ordered Iktómi's home to be felled.

When the sun disappeared and the moon rose into the sky, Iktómi prepared for the wolf pack's arrival. Clouds covered the night sky, blocking out the stars and the moon. The only light came from the fire burning at the center of the village. Iktómi spat at the Lakota, knowing the wood keeping the flames alive came from his own tree. After most of the tribe were fast asleep, the wolves finally stalked to the edge of the village. They looked angry and merciless.

The wolves charged forward, overwhelming the guards and keeping an eye out for danger. They stormed through the village, tearing down teepees and ripping the Lakota apart. The Wolf Chief thundered into the Lakota chief's teepee and tore out his throat, much to Iktómi's delight. He even got involved, changing into his wolf form and getting his revenge on the man who had chopped down his tree. When the pack had finished their grisly work, they met back up at the center of the village.

"Chief, I saw no weapons or hunting gear in this place," a young wolf said. "Their horses do not look like they are prepared to ride at dawn."

"I saw none of that, either," a she-wolf added. "The only blades were those used to carve totem poles."

"You mean to say you believe the Lakota were not going to attack us?" the Wolf Chief asked. Nearly all of his pack agreed that there were no signs that the tribe presented any danger to them. The Wolf Chief turned to the black wolf and growled, "Did you trick us, Iktómi? Was everything you told me a lie?"

"They destroyed my home and deserved this fate," Iktómi stated proudly. "You should not feel bad about killing them."

The Wolf Chief snarled at him angrily. "What do you mean they destroyed your home? Do you not live wherever you spin your webs?"

"I spun my web in an old oak tree," Iktómi replied. "They cut it down."

"We have lived in peace with the Lakota for years," the Wolf told him. "As long as we kept our distance, they left us alone. Now, you have made us slaughter our neighbors for the offense of chopping down a tree? You do not stay in one place for more than a few days. As you would be going somewhere else soon anyway, why did you not simply leave?"

"Why should I have to leave the tree? They could have chosen another one to cut down."

"Perhaps they should have," the Wolf said. "But tricking us into killing them was not a reasonable response. You have not just caused harm to them – you have harmed my pack as well. Now we will live with the shame of knowing we killed these people for no good reason."

"It is too late to take it back," Iktómi pointed out. "Why feel guilty for something that is already done?"

"Because what we did was not justified. What you tricked us into doing was murder." The Wolf Chief lowered his head and looked like he was ready to spring at any moment. "You will pay for this evil you brought upon us!"

Iktómi laughed and transformed into a swallow, flapping his wings as he flew toward the sky. To his surprise, the Wolf Chief leaped into the air and snatched Iktómi by his legs. The Wolf's fangs bit clean through them, and while Iktómi escaped, he was deeply wounded. When he found a new tree in which to spin his web, he was a spider with only six legs. Iktómi remembered the Wolf Chief's words every time he felt the pain from his wounds. He realized the Wolf was right. While his actions were evil, the Wolf could have killed him, but instead, he only took a part of him. The punishment did not go further than the crime.

Young Man Afraid of His Horses (Tashun-Kakokipa)[51]

Chapter Round-Up Activity

Sometimes, you'll hear information that doesn't sound quite right. Can you figure out the difference between real and fake facts? Think about everything you've read in this chapter and see if you can tell whether the following statements are true or false:

1. The Lakota live in longhouses.

2. The Hunkpapa fought on the side of the United States during the American Indian Wars.

3. Seven subtribes make up the Lakota.

4. The Sans Arc people marked their arrows so nobody else could claim the buffalo they killed.

5. Lakota boys could join in on the buffalo hunts as young as ten years old.

6. Sitting Bull was a member of the Hunkpapa subtribe of the Lakota.

7. Iktómi is the name of a powerful wolf spirit in Lakota mythology.

8. Some members of the Sioux Nation originally lived in the Great Plains before being forced to move to reservations.

9. The Lakota targeted the buffalo at the head of a stampeding herd.

10. Crazy Horse fought against the United States Army during the Battle of Gettysburg.

Answers

1. False
2. True
3. True
4. False
5. True
6. True
7. False
8. True
9. False
10. False

Chapter 3: Pueblo Spirits: Kachinas and the Art of Storytelling

The Pueblo people are Native Americans who live in the Southwestern part of the United States, mostly in New Mexico, Arizona, Texas, and Colorado. Tribes that are considered Puebloans include the Hopi, Acoma, Taos, Isleta, and Zuni. They are known as the Pueblo people because they traditionally live in adobe structures called pueblos. Living in the dry, arid heat of the southwestern deserts means that getting enough rain to support the growing of crops is very important, and the Pueblo tribes have many customs and rituals to encourage rainfall. Rain dances and kachinas dedicated to bringing the rain are popular across every Puebloan tribe.

Kachinas

In the religious beliefs of the Pueblo people, a "kachina" is the name used for cultural spirit beings who serve as protectors and help bring good fortune to the community. The kachinas have three parts: a supernatural spirit, a kachina dancer, and a kachina doll. The kachina dancers perform dance rituals during Pueblo ceremonies, wearing masks and body paint to help channel the kachina spirits. Kachina dolls are carved wooden figures painted with bright colors given to Pueblo children. The kachina dolls help them learn about the different kachina spirits, allowing Pueblo children to recognize the spirits on sight.

The kachina spirits are believed to be the ancestors of the Pueblo people, and they are said to live in the underworld for half the year while spending the other half on Earth with their descendants. Puebloans depend on kachinas to aid the community by bringing rainfall, encouraging crop growth, keeping family members safe, and blessing sources of food. Kachinas can be represented by symbols of animals, cultural objects, or important members of the tribe, like a chief or priestess. Many Puebloans keep kachina dolls in their homes to ask for protection from a specific kachina spirit and teach their family about the kachinas important to them.

The Little Lost Kachina Doll

One day, a child of the Hopi tribe was sent by his parents to fetch water from the river. He followed the path from his village to the river's edge, but a terrible thunderstorm rolled in while he was filling his buckets. The rain poured down and made it hard to see, while the wind whipped around him, making it hard to move. Knowing there was no way he would be able to get back home through the storm, he was forced to find shelter in a nearby cave. After sitting his water buckets down near the entrance, he explored the cave while waiting out the storm.

Near the back of the cave, the child noticed a tiny, strange-looking figure lying on the ground. He picked it up and inspected it, turning it over in his hand. It was made of wood from a Douglas fir, had a painted blue face, a red leather tunic trimmed with white fur, and two large black bird wings. The child recognized it as a kachina doll, almost identical to the one his family had hanging up in their pueblo. His parents had taught him that this kachina was known as the Crow Mother, who was a protector of young children.

A crack of thunder boomed outside, and a flash of lightning lit up the cave. To the child's horror, he saw a red-eyed coyote snarling at him. It bared its razor-sharp fangs at him and let out a howl. The child was frozen in fear, unable to move or run for his life. All he could do was clutch the kachina doll to his chest. Suddenly, a gust of wind filled the cave, swirling around, lifting the dirt and creating a small tornado. As quickly as it appeared, the wind came to a halt, and from the cloud of dirt it left behind, a large figure emerged.

The child looked on in awe as the figure stepped forward to challenge the coyote. She looked exactly like the Crow Mother kachina doll but was almost twice as tall as him. Her wings flapped and forced the coyote back.

It howled at the Crow Mother and dug its claws into the ground. Despite its best efforts, it couldn't fight back and turned to flee from the cave, disappearing into the storm. The Crow Mother turned to face the child and laid her hand on his shoulder, removing the chill from his soul and filling him with warmth. There was another blast of thunder and a flash of lightning so bright the child was forced to cover his eyes.

When the child could see again, the Crow Mother was gone. Even the kachina doll he'd been holding had disappeared. Luckily, the rain stopped falling, and the child was able to leave the cave with the buckets of water he'd filled at the river. He hurried back home to his village, checking over his shoulder to make sure the coyote hadn't followed him. After reaching his family's pueblo, he gave the water buckets to his parents and went straight to the Crow Mother kachina doll hanging on the wall. He bowed his head to the figure and whispered, "Thank you for protecting me."

The Zuni Rain Dance Ceremony

The sun streamed in through Lucita's bedroom window and woke her up. After wiping the sleep from her eyes, she looked at the calendar and saw that it was the 19th of August, the day of her tribe's annual rain dance ceremony! She leaped out of bed, more excited than usual. This was the first year she would be allowed to participate in the ceremony. Leading up to the rain dance, she double-checked that everything was in order, not wanting anything to go wrong.

When the time came for the ceremony to begin, Lucita emerged from her home dressed in the traditional clothing all women wear to perform the rain dance; a long black dress with a white embroidered underskirt that showed a few inches at the bottom, a bright Spanish shawl with alternating red and yellow colors in an arrowhead pattern, two square over-shawls, one colored black and the other white, both having a red and white striped border and an ornately-decorated kachina mask that was shaped like an eagle. No part of her body or face was showing beneath her outfit besides her bare feet.

Lucita joined the tribe members and participated in the ceremony at the center of her village. She got into the line behind the other women, standing about four feet away from the line of men. The high priest of the tribe came out and offered a blessing to the kachina spirits before kicking off the ceremony. Lucita and the other kachina dancers began their rain dance routine. She followed their rhythm, stepping with her left foot, then a little further with her right. Slowly, the rain dancers inched their way forward, moving in groups of three around two sides of the four-sided quadrangle of the village center.

Although the male rain dancers had fiercer energy in their steps, the female dancers moved more gracefully. Lucita felt like she was ebbing and flowing along the current of a river, swirling around in her kachina costume. The energy of the spirits filled her body, and it was as if they were controlling her motions. Every step she took and dance move she executed wasn't just her calling out to the heavens for the rain to fall. Lucita could see her ancestors and the tribe elders, who had long since passed. They all joined in with the dancers, amplifying the call of the spirits within.

The dancers sang the traditional songs of their tribe, honoring those who came before and those who would arrive in the future. Every dancer got a chance to add their own verse, improvising the lyrics to make a personal appeal to the kachina spirits. When it was Lucita's turn, she knew exactly what she wanted to say. In a powerful voice that came from deep in her soul, she cried out, "We see the corn and the wheat and the grain, we give thanks to the spirits for giving us these gifts! The rivers, sun, and clouds that carry the rain, we give thanks to the wellspring of life on this Earth!"

The rain dance ceremony ended, and it was time for the celebration to begin. The tribe had prepared a great feast to honor the harvest and welcome the autumn months. Many in the village approached Lucita to compliment her on her performance. She wore a smile that stretched from ear to ear, proud of the fact that her first rain dance was a success. When all the food had been eaten, and the cups were bone dry, the stars and the moon came out to play. By the time Lucita returned to her bed, she was ready for a good night's sleep.

As she drifted off, she heard a soft pitter-patter on her roof. It grew louder, battering the roof of her home. Looking out the window, she saw the torrent of rain showering down on the world. The tribe's rain dance had worked; the crops would be well-fed that night! Lucita was very satisfied with that outcome. She had given her heart and soul to the dance, and the spirits accepted this offering as payment for bringing the rain. Now that the ceremony was over, she looked forward to doing it again when another year had passed.

Chapter Round-Up Activity

How well do you remember the tales told in this chapter? Can you finish these stories in your own words? Take a look at the following sections of the tales you've just read and try to fill in the missing parts (If you're using an e-reader or reading in an e-book format, you can write your responses in a notebook):

1. When the time came for the ceremony to begin, Lucita emerged from her home dressed in the traditional clothing all women wear to perform the rain dance:

   _____

   _____

   _____

   _____

   _____

2. Near the back of the cave, the child noticed a tiny, strange-looking figure lying on the ground. He picked it up and inspected it, turning it over in his hand. It was made of wood from a Douglas fir, had a painted blue face, a red leather tunic trimmed with white fur, and two large black bird wings. The child recognized it as

   _____

   _____

   _____

   _____

3. The kachina spirits are believed to be the ancestors of the Pueblo people, and they are said to live in

   _____

   _____

   _____

   _____

4. The dancers sang the traditional songs of their tribe, honoring those who came before and those who would arrive in the future. Every dancer got a chance to add their own verse, improvising the lyrics to make a personal appeal to the kachina spirits. When it was Lucita's turn, she knew exactly what she wanted to say. In a powerful voice that came from deep in her soul, she cried out,

_____

_____

_____

_____

_____

5. When the child could see again, the Crow Mother was gone. Even the kachina doll he'd been holding had disappeared. Luckily, the rain stopped falling, and the child could leave the cave with the buckets of water he'd filled at the river. He hurried back home to his village, checking over his shoulder to make sure the coyote didn't follow him. After reaching his family's pueblo, he gave the water buckets to his parents and went straight to the Crow Mother kachina doll hanging on the wall. He

_____

_____

_____

_____

_____

Chapter 4: Cherokees: The Trail of Tears and Resistance

The Cherokee Nation is a tribe of Native Americans who lived in the Southeastern Woodlands of the United States, mostly in Virginia, North Carolina, South Carolina, Georgia, Tennessee, and Alabama. After the Indian Removal Act of 1830, the Cherokee were forced to endure a long and deadly trek from their homelands to the Indian Territory west of the Mississippi River. This event was known as the Trail of Tears, and it involved the forced relocation of five major tribes, which the United States called the "Five Civilized Tribes," including the Cherokee, Chickasaw, Muscogee, Choctaw, and Seminole tribes.

The Seal of the Cherokee Nation.[53]

The Trail of Tears

The Trail of Tears lasted from 1830 (when the Indian Removal Act was signed into law by United States President Andrew Jackson) until 1850. During those twenty years, over 60,000 Native Americans from the Five Civilized Tribes were forcibly moved from their native lands to the Indian Territory, which was designated specifically for the Native Americans. No matter which part of the country the Native Americans originally lived in, they were sent west of the Mississippi River to a portion of what are now the states of Arkansas and Oklahoma. The journey from their homelands to the Indian Territory was dangerous for those forced to make it, stretching across more than 5,000 miles, and between 13,200 and 16,700 people died from disease and warfare along the way.

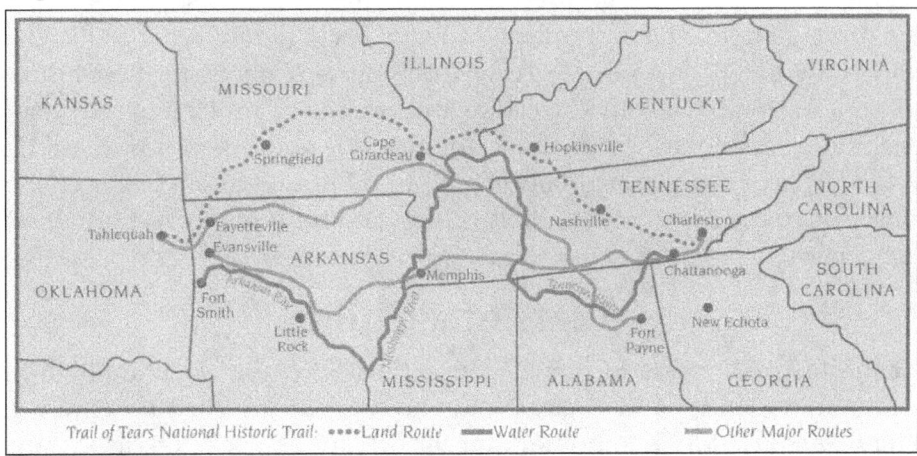

The Trail of Tears.[53]

Not all Native Americans simply accepted their forced removal and relocation. Some groups fought back against the United States government, with many resistance movements erupting into violence. The Seminole tribe refused to submit to the Indian Removal Act, having already been fighting against being forced onto reservations. The Seminole Wars first broke out in 1816, and they continued all the way until 1858. Smaller collections of other tribes also resisted, including about 100 Cherokees. Despite their best efforts, they were unable to stop the Trail of Tears from happening, and, in the end, all their land was taken by the United States.

Cherokee Culture

The Cherokee Nation was traditionally made up of "red towns" and "white towns." The red towns were meant for warriors and had a supreme war chief as their top leader. The white towns were for the peaceful tribe members, and they were led by a supreme peace chief. The Cherokee living in red towns were known for their elaborate war ceremonies, while the white towns gave wrongdoers a safe place to live. Together, the two types of towns provided the Cherokees with the ability to fight and defend their people and places where those who wanted to avoid conflict could go.

A major part of Cherokee culture was the weaving of baskets and making of pottery. They grew corn (called "maize"), squash, and beans to feed their people. Their hunters brought back hides, furs, and antlers from bears, deer, and elk to create furniture and decorate their homes. Those homes were mostly log cabins with tree bark roofs, and they had a single door, a smoke hole in the roof, and no windows in the walls. The average Cherokee town had between 30 to 60 homes and a larger council house where the tribe could hold meetings and burn the sacred fire during ceremonies.

Tears of a Child

For the first nine years of her life, Inola had lived with her family in the vibrant green lands of Georgia. Now, she was being forced to leave it all behind: her friends, her home, and all the spirits she'd come to know while wandering through the grasslands and forests. She said goodbye to the jagged rocks, the towering trees, the babbling brook, and the soft dirt that she'd come to know so well. Inola could feel the sadness around her as she bid them all farewell. Even the skies wept for her. The raindrops splattered against the ground as her family began their journey to the new lands where they would live.

"Mother, I do not want to go," Inola said sadly.

"We have to go, child," her mother replied. "The White Men have threatened to burn down our homes and shoot us with their guns if we do not follow their orders."

Everything Inola's family owned was being carried on their backs. They had to leave behind their furniture and decorations, including her favorite painted pot. It was too big to fit in their packs and would have taken up too much room. Her father and older brother carried most of their belongings, but her mother was hauling her fair share of the burden. Even Inola had a pack strapped to her back, filled with a handful of her own things. She hugged her corn husk doll to her chest and tried to ignore the aching in her legs. Her mother warned her they would need to walk ten miles daily to reach the Indian Territory within four months. She couldn't imagine having to walk that far, but she tried to look at it as a grand adventure.

Many other Cherokee families were traveling from one side of the Mississippi River to the other. Some had wagons, but most were forced to go on foot, like Inola's family. Her father and brother hunted for animals, while Inola and her mother picked berries and nuts. As they traveled along the trail, they discovered it became harder to find food since so many other Cherokees were walking the same path and taking food from the same places. Luckily, her father was one of the tribe's best hunters, and he always managed to track and kill something for them to eat.

The rain made the ground muddy, and Inola had trouble walking through it. Her mother held her hand and helped her along the way, but it slowed the family down. They watched the other Cherokees pass by them, and Inola felt guilty that she was making the journey take longer than it should be. Her father set up a basic camp for them at night, but it was only a small fire and blankets made from the bear he killed while out hunting three years ago. There were only two blankets, so Inola's father and brother had only the campfire to keep them warm.

A week into the trip, the family reached Fort Payne in Alabama. The White Men from the United States Army herded the Cherokees like cattle through the fort, sending them on their way. Inola and her family spent the night camped outside the fort, packed with hundreds of her people, seeking to find some extra food that the soldiers had stored away. A few dozen soldiers stepped over the Cherokees as they gave out some bread and corn. One soldier took pity on Inola's brother and gave him a small blanket made of woven wool. The next day, they followed the other members of their tribe as the soldiers pushed them to continue on their journey.

Inola's family headed north, crossing the border into Tennessee. The land became harder to walk on, as hills began to rise and fall as they left Alabama. It seemed to her that the weather was harsher, and it was getting colder at night. She felt tired all the time now, as her entire life was nothing but walking, eating, and sleeping. However, her sleep was far from restful, and she no longer woke up feeling refreshed. As they got closer to

Memphis, Inola's brother developed a nasty cough. He got weaker and weaker, to the point that his mother began carrying part of his load. It wasn't long before he could barely keep himself upright, and the family was forced to leave behind part of their precious few belongings.

Seven miles outside of Memphis, Inola's family got caught in a snowstorm that rolled through the area. They took shelter in a small cave to wait out the storm. In the morning, after the snow had stopped falling, Inola's father dug them out with his hands. When he cleared a path to let them escape, two of his fingers were completely blue and swollen. He couldn't feel them anymore, and his wife realized he'd got frostbite. Not wanting to delay their travels more than they had to, Inola's father woke her brother up so they could go.

"Wake up, boy – we must leave this cave," her father said. He nudged his son with his good hand, but Inola's brother would not get up. Her brother didn't move, either. In fact, he wasn't moving at all. To her horror, her father announced to the family, "Our boy is dead."

He dug a grave for Inola's brother inside the cave since the soil outside was frozen and too hard to break. Since her brother didn't bring anything that was just his own, they buried him with the blanket given to him by the soldier at the fort. Her mother wanted it gone anyway because she blamed it for getting him sick. There was no feast, no celebration of his life, and they remained at his graveside only long enough to offer a short prayer. Inola's father assured his mother that the spirits would understand. If they didn't leave soon, they would all die in that cave.

Trudging through the snow was a miserable experience for Inola. She and her mother kept their blankets wrapped around themselves, but her father had only his regular clothing to protect him. He led the way, pushing aside as much of the snow as he could to make it easier for the rest of his family to walk. Inola carefully stepped into her father's footprints to avoid sinking her feet into the snow. As the hours passed, she noticed his footprints were getting closer together, and she could tell he was exhausted. However, he refused to stop until they reached the city.

The family finally made it to Memphis. Inola was in awe, looking up at the large buildings and factories chugging thick black smoke from the metal smokestacks. She tried to imagine what kind of fires could create smoke like that. She knew the only large buildings with large fires were the lodges where great council meetings took place, so she assumed they must serve the same purpose for the White Men. Although she had hoped her family would get to spend the night inside one of the many buildings that littered the city, they didn't have any money, and the White Men refused to barter. They were forced to sleep in an encampment with their fellow Cherokees and other tribes.

Inola and her family spent several days in the city waiting for the snow to melt. She watched the White Men in their strange, heavy clothing rush around all day. People streamed into the factories and came back out at night looking red-faced and dirty. Many of them went directly to the taverns, which were filled with a mixture of laughter and shouts. Some of the White Men ended up getting into scuffles outside the taverns, and Inola witnessed one man get shot with a gun. She couldn't understand how they lived in a place like that. It was crowded, loud, and suffocating. No matter how hard she tried, she couldn't feel the presence of the spirits anywhere.

After noticing another group of people she'd never seen before, Inola asked her mother, "Who are those people with skin darker than ours?"

"They are slaves. They are owned by the White Men," her mother explained.

"How can the White Men own them?" Inola asked in confusion. "We are all born free, so we can live in balance with nature."

"The White Men take many things that do not belong to them," her mother said. "That includes the freedom of the dark-skinned people from across the sea."

When it came time to leave the city, Inola's father had managed to get some food to take with them. His fingers hadn't healed from the frostbite, and he feared that he wouldn't be able to draw arrows in his bow as well as he did before. That would make it harder for him to hunt, and fewer things grew in the harsher winters of these lands. The family returned to the trail and soon crossed the Mississippi River into Arkansas. They had to wait almost an entire day to use the White Men's ferries to take them across the raging waters, as it was too deep and dangerous to ford on foot.

Their trip through Arkansas stretched on for weeks. When they ran out of food, Inola's father went hunting despite his injured fingers. Upon his return, he apologized for only managing to kill a small rabbit. Still, they were grateful to have anything to eat. Inola's father took only a single bite of meat before handing it to her, and then he went to sleep. In the morning, he looked tired and weaker than she'd ever seen him, but he insisted that he was fine. However, when they loaded their packs, he couldn't lift his own, and they were again forced to leave some of their belongings behind.

Inola's family reached another place settled by the White Men called Evansville, but it wasn't anything like Memphis. This was a small trading post town, and to her father's surprise, the owner of the trading post was actually willing to barter. Instead of giving the trading post owner money in exchange for food, her father traded a few of their remaining belongings for it. Inola's mother had to give up her bear skin blanket, as it was the only item the trader really seemed to want. That at least got them plenty of food to last the rest of their journey, as long as there were no more delays.

Only a few days after leaving the trading post, Inola's father became nervous, constantly looking over his shoulder and scanning their surroundings like he did while hunting. Her parents kept whispering to each other, but she couldn't hear what they were saying. When the family was camped out for the night, her father refused to sleep and held his bow across his lap. At some point, she was awakened by shouting and opened her eyes to find three Chickasaw men rushing toward their camp. Her father was firing arrows at them, but he could not hit his marks. They soon reached him, and although he fought as well as he could, they overpowered him in the end. One Chickasaw plunged a knife into his neck, and they grabbed the family's stockpile of food before disappearing into the night.

There was nothing Inola's mother could do to save her husband, and by morning, he was dead. She and her daughter dug a grave for him and buried him with his bow. As with Inola's brother, they didn't feast and had nothing to celebrate. As soon as they offered prayers to the spirits, they packed up what little they had left and could carry. Inola's mother had tucked a small bit of food away in her own pack, which the Chickasaw thieves managed to overlook. They set out again, their family now half the size it was when they left their home.

Inola and her mother moved slower than before and stopped more often. Her mother insisted on giving their remaining food to her daughter while keeping only a few bites for herself. Inola watched her mother wasting away before her eyes, but her mother's spirit was fierce. They had made it to the Indian Territory. They were only a couple of days away from Tahlequah, the new capital of the Cherokee Nation. The moment Inola spotted the large village in the distance, she shouted for joy.

Her mother smiled weakly and said, "Go, child. You can make it from here on your own. Do not wait for me."

"Why must I go alone?" Inola asked. "We are so close. Our people will give us food and shelter."

Her mother never answered. She collapsed to the ground, and no matter what Inola did, she couldn't wake her back up. Refusing to leave her mother, she sat there on the ground for hours, pleading with her mother to wake up. A pair of Cherokee hunters stumbled upon them. They knew immediately that Inola's mother was dead. The hunters were kind to Inola and helped her bury her mother's body, then took her to Tahlequah with them. They took her to the village's chief, and he listened to her tell him about all that her family had suffered and endured throughout their journey. When Inola had finished speaking, she burst out crying. She couldn't hold in the sorrow any longer.

"We will take care of you, child, for you are one of us," the chief assured her. "This new land is different, but we are still Cherokee. We do not abandon our own."

"Thank you, chief," Inola said between sobs.

The chief's wife took Inola by the hand and led her away to find something to eat and somewhere to sleep. The chief sighed sadly as he watched Inola go. She was far from the first to tell him such a tale, and he feared many more would come.

He turned to his shaman advisor and stated, "Those of our people do not need to follow a trail of footprints to find this new land. They only need to follow the trail of tears we have left behind."

Chapter Round-Up Activity

How much were you able to learn from this chapter? Can you pick out the right answer from multiple choices? See if you can find the correct response to the following questions:

1. What year did President Andrew Jackson sign the Indian Removal Act into law?

    a.   1848

    b.   1830

    c.   1819

    d.   1854

2. What is part of the Cherokee people's funeral customs?

    a.   They bury their dead in graves

    b.   They have a feast and celebration

    c.   They leave belongings in the graves

    d.   All of the above

3. How many windows were in a typical Cherokee cabin?

    a.   4

    b.   0

    c.   2

    d.   6

4. Which tribe was NOT considered part of the "Five Civilized Tribes?"

    a.   Cherokee

    b.   Muscogee

    c.   Lakota

    d.   Seminole

5. About how many Native Americans were forced to endure the Trail of Tears?

    a.   60,000

    b.   45,000

    c.   100,000

    d.   86,000

6. What was the name of the Cherokee capital in the Indian Territory?

    a. Memphis

    b. New Echota

    c. Tahlequah

    d. Fort Payne

7. What type of crop was NOT grown by the Cherokee people?

    a. Potatoes

    b. Maize

    c. Squash

    d. Beans

8. Which two colors were used for the Cherokee's war and peace towns?

    a. Blue and Yellow

    b. Red and White

    c. White and Green

    d. Red and Yellow

9. What future state was the Indian Territory located in?

    a. Nevada

    b. Georgia

    c. Kansas

    d. Oklahoma

10. How many homes were in a typical Cherokee village?

    a. 40 to 50

    b. 25 to 35

    c. 15 to 45

    d. 30 to 60

Answers

1. b.
2. d.
3. b.
4. c.
5. a.
6. c.
7. a.
8. b.
9. d.
10. d.

Chapter 5: Iroquois (Haudenosaunee) Confederacy: The Great Law of Peace

The Iroquois or Haudenosaunee Confederacy was originally made up of five tribes, and after 1722, six tribes. They were also known as the Five or Six Nations by the English colonists. The Confederacy was different from other tribes or alliances at the time because they had a system in place to give each member tribe a voice in the decisions they made. Rather than having a single chief, each tribe voted for which members would get a seat on the Grand Council, and those elected members then represented their tribe in discussions and decisions made by the Council.

Before 1722, the Iroquois Confederacy was made up of the Seneca, Cayuga, Oneida, Onondaga, and Mohawk tribes. In 1722, they added the Tuscarora tribe to the Confederacy. At the height of their power and influence, the Iroquois' lands stretched from Ontario and Quebec in Canada to the Northeastern United States, going as far south as the Allegheny Mountains in Virginia. They also held territory in the states of New York, Pennsylvania, West Virginia, Ohio, and Kentucky. The Iroquois mostly lived along the shores of lakes and the banks of rivers, such as the Great Lakes and the Ohio River.

Flag of the Iroquois Confederacy.[54]

Longhouses

Longhouses were an important part of Iroquois culture. The name they used for themselves was "Haudenosaunee," which means "people of the longhouse." The Iroquois lived in longhouses made from wooden poles, which were created by cutting down tree saplings and using fire to remove all the moisture from them so they would become harder. They sharpened one end of the poles so they could drive them into the ground like stakes, securing the walls of their homes. The roofs were made from poles bent into arcs with grass and leaves covering the top, and both the walls and roof used poles set from the front to the back of the longhouse to keep them sturdy.

An average longhouse was 80 feet long, 18 feet wide, and 18 feet high. They were meant to shelter many families, sometimes as many as twenty, in a single longhouse. Most of these families were related in some way through the female members, such as sons and daughters of the same mother, grandchildren of the same grandmother, or the families of sisters. There were also larger longhouses built to serve as meeting places to hold celebrations and discuss tribal matters. When it came time for tribes to elect representatives to sit on the Grand Council of the Iroquois Confederacy and speak for their people, the voting often happened in the larger longhouses.

Wampum Belts

A wampum is a type of shell bead shaped like a tube that was used by the Iroquois to create belts and jewelry. These shell beads could be many different colors, and the Iroquois developed a system that allowed them to use specific combinations of colored wampum to represent words and ideas. Wampum belts were woven with colored bead shells with designs that could be read by anyone who knew the wampum language system. The Iroquois used wampum belts to keep records of events and the treaties they made.

The Great Peacemaker

Long ago, before the White Men came to the New World, there were many Native American tribes living throughout the unspoiled lands. However, not all of them got along, and there were five tribes in the northeastern part of the New World that were constantly at war. The Seneca, Cayuga, Oneida, Onondaga, and Mohawk tribes seemed to hate each other. Whenever there was a short time of peace, it soon ended, and they were back to fighting. The people just accepted that this was how things were, believing it was how things would always be.

Far to the north, a tribe known as the Huron lived apart from the other tribes. There was a woman among them whom the others found strange, and none of the men wanted to marry her. The women of the tribe bullied her, and the men made fun of her, causing her to go off on her own. Since she was not married and lived away from the rest of her tribe, she was shocked when she woke up one day to find that she was pregnant. She thanked the spirits for this miracle because it meant she would no longer be alone.

After giving birth, the Huron woman named her baby Dekanawida, which meant "two river currents flowing together." She chose that name because she strongly believed that he was going to grow up to do something important and sit at the point where the destinies of others would meet. Dekanawida wasn't raised like the other children of the Huron tribe. His mother didn't want him to be a warrior. She wanted him to be a force for peace. Whenever he spoke to the other people of his tribe, they looked down on him for trying to get them to abandon their warlike ways.

When Dekanawida got older, he truly understood why his mother preached peace over war. He went south to hunt for food and stumbled upon a battlefield after a fight between the Mohawks and Oneidas. What he found horrified him, as he'd never seen so much death before in his life. There was a Mohawk warrior collecting war trophies, and Dekanawida asked him why the two tribes had fought.

"I do not remember," the Mohawk warrior said. "That is just the way it is."

Later, Dekanawida caught up to an Oneida warrior limping back to his village. Dekanawida asked him the same question.

"I do not remember," answered the Oneida warrior. "That is just the way it is."

Dekanawida couldn't believe that the tribes were willing to kill each other when they didn't even know why they wanted the other side to die. They had simply become so used to war that the idea of *not* killing each other never entered their minds. However, he also knew that his message of peace would not be received very well if he approached the tribes alone. His own tribe dismissed every attempt he made to teach them about peace. There was no way he'd be successful with the rival tribes.

When Dekanawida reached adulthood, his mother urged him to leave home and fulfill his destiny. He was doubtful that he could be successful in his mission to bring peace to the tribes, but his mother believed in him. She insisted that he was meant to do great things with his life and that he would someday become important in helping his people in some way.

That night, his mother went outside to meditate beneath a nearby tree. In the morning, she was gone, and Dekanawida searched far and wide, trying to find her. She was nowhere to be found, so he cut down the tree and made it into a canoe when he returned home. He dragged the canoe down to the river and got in, traveling south to the lands of the five rival tribes. Dekanawida was determined to follow through with his mission and make his mother proud. He came up with the Great Law of Peace, a way for enemies to become allies by using peaceful discussions to settle their conflicts instead of going to war.

Reaching the lands of the rival tribes, Dekanawida did his best to spread his message of peace. They laughed at him as he expected, calling him a coward for not wanting to be a warrior, and sent him away. Each of the five tribes gave him the same cold treatment, and he quickly lost hope in ever completing his mission. While journeying across the lands, he stopped to rest at the home of a woman who was known for taking in warriors from every tribe. The warriors would get food and sleep safely because the woman refused to allow them to fight when they were under her roof.

Dekanawida recognized that the woman shared a similar outlook to him. They spoke for hours, with Dekanawida explaining his vision for all the tribes to live in peace. He was inspired by the way she got the enemy warriors to not kill each other when they were in her home, and he told her that he wanted to build a longhouse where the tribes could meet and talk out their problems around the fire, just like they ate and slept in peace around the fire in her home. The woman really liked that idea and promised to support Dekanawida's mission in any way she could. She also changed her name to Jigonhsasee, which meant "new face," to show her devotion to his vision of peace.

Not long after leaving Jigonhsasee's home, Dekanawida spotted a cabin that sat alone in the mountains. He hiked up to the cabin, wanting to meet the person who lived there. The owner of the home was away when he arrived, but there was something cooking in a pot on the fire in the cabin. Dekanawida climbed onto the roof and looked down the smoke hole to see what it was. He was sickened when he discovered that the cabin's owner was cooking people. This was the home of a truly evil person, but Dekanawida thought that if he could convert the man to his vision for peace, he could convince anyone that peace was better than war.

The cabin's owner returned home and went to check on his food. He looked down into the pot, expecting to see his own face reflected in the boiling water. Instead, he saw the reflection of Dekanawida's face staring down the smoke hole. The face he saw didn't look evil like his face, but it looked beautiful, wise, and strong. The man mistook it for his own face, thinking the spirits had transformed him and removed the evil from his soul. However, the face disappeared, and when he looked in the pot again, he saw only his own ugly reflection. This made him feel ashamed, and he was saddened to realize how terrible he'd become.

Hiawatha by Thomas Eakins.[55]

Dekanawida entered the cabin, and the man was surprised to see the face from the cooking pot again. It made him feel even more ashamed that he would never get to know what it was like to be anything other than evil.

"Are you an avenging spirit who has come to kill me for the evil I have done?" the man asked.

"No. I do not believe in killing anyone, no matter how evil they might be," Dekanawida replied. "Tell me your name so I may speak to you properly."

"My name is Hiawatha. I was once an Onondaga, but when they found out about the evil I had done, they sent me away to live alone in the mountains. They forced me to leave my family behind. I have become such a terrible man; my wife and children would not recognize me if they saw me today."

"Hiawatha, I know you have done many evil things," Dekanawida said. "But you can change your ways if you want to."

"I want to change my ways," Hiawatha insisted. "I am tired of having this evil in my soul. I want to see my family again. Tell me what I must do, and I will do it. I no longer wish to hurt others. I want to be like you."

"Then you must spread my message of peace. Return to your people and give them the Great Law of Peace."

Dekanawida told Hiawatha everything about his plans and ideas for a peaceful future. Hiawatha agreed to Dekanawida's terms and returned to his people to spread the message of peace. Dekanawida set off to find more who were willing to accept his vision, feeling more positive about his chances after having convinced Hiawatha to change his evil ways. The men headed out in separate directions – Hiawatha to the Onondaga village and Dekanawida to the Mohawk village.

When Hiawatha reached his old tribe, they weren't happy to see him. He was told that after he was sent away, an evil chief named Tadodaho had taken over. The Onondaga's new chief could use magic, and his body and mind were twisted by the evil spells he cast. Tadodaho had snakes instead of hair – and snakes coming out of his fingers! Hiawatha tried to spread Dekanawida's message of peace, calling the tribe together and suggesting they form a council to rule the tribe instead of a chief. Tadodaho was furious at Hiawatha for trying to take away his power, and he killed the man's wife and three daughters with his magic. Filled with grief at learning about the fate of his family, Hiawatha left the village, wandering the wilderness while mourning his lost loved ones.

Meanwhile, Dekanawida came to the village of the Mohawks and spoke about the Great Law of Peace. They refused to believe they could survive without fighting against the other tribes. They challenged him to prove that the spirits supported his message. He accepted their challenge and climbed a tall tree growing beside a deep gorge. Looking over the edge, he saw the ground was hundreds of feet down. Falling into the gorge was a sure way to die, but the Mohawks told him that if the spirits were on his side, he would survive. They cut down the tree with Dekanawida still in it and watched it fall into the gorge. It appeared to them that the spirits weren't with him, and they returned to their village to prepare for war.

The next morning, the Mohawks were shocked when Dekanawida returned to the village unharmed. Since he survived the fall into the gorge, they decided the spirits must be on his side and support his vision. They finally accepted his message of peace and converted from their warlike ways to become a tribe that solved their problems without violence. After living with the Mohawks and helping them change their ways, a scout found the wandering Hiawatha and brought him back to the village. He explained to Dekanawida about what happened at the Onondaga village and begged Dekanawida to take away his pain. Dekanawida performed a ritual to help Hiawatha and began to chant.

"I wipe away tears from thy face, using the white fawn skin of pity," he said. "I make it daylight for thee. I beautify the sky. Now shall thou do thy thinking in peace."

All those who watched Dekanawida's ritual were amazed to see it work. Hiawatha's grief and pain were lifted from his soul. The pair decided to visit the other tribes to convince them that peace was the right path. The Mohawk's newly-elected leaders went with them, hoping that by showing their rival tribes they had accepted the message of peace, the tribes would do the same. With the Mohawks' support, Dekanawida got the Oneida and Cayuga to join their mission and give peace a chance to improve their lives.

The Seneca were in the middle of a conflict within their tribe when the messengers of peace came to their village. Word had spread of the other tribes laying down their weapons and giving up their wars. Half of the Senecas wanted to join with the peaceful tribes, while the other half felt it was nothing but a trick. It looked like the Senecas were about to go to war with themselves when the outsiders interrupted them. Dekanawida spoke about the Great Law of Peace, but the half of the tribe who still wanted to fight weren't sure it would work. During their discussions, there was a solar eclipse, and seeing the moon block out the sun's light was taken as a sign from the spirits to accept Dekanawida's vision.

Four of the five tribes had joined each other to live peacefully, but the Onondaga remained their enemy. Dekanawida, Hiawatha, and the leaders from the other four tribes returned to the Onondaga village to confront Tadodaho together. When the group arrived at the Onondaga village, the evil chief tried to turn them away. Still, his people were impressed that Dekanawida had convinced enemies to become allies. Dekanawida told Hiawatha to comb the snakes out of Tadodaho's hair while he performed the same ritual he'd used to help Hiawatha. In the end, they removed the evil from Tadodaho, straightening his twisted body and mind as he gave up his evil ways.

With the Onondaga now joined with their alliance, Dekanawida prepared to give a speech in which he would suggest the five tribes combine into a single tribe. They all shared the same ancestors and spoke similar languages, so they had much more in common than they originally believed. However, Dekanawida could not speak publicly because he had a stutter that got worse when he gave speeches to large groups. Hiawatha was skilled at public speaking, so he addressed the tribes in Dekanawida's place. When Hiawatha's speech was over, the five tribes agreed to make their alliance official and created the Iroquois Confederacy.

Now that the Iroquois were a single tribe, they needed to organize it and how their leadership would work. Dekanawida brought in Jigonhsasee – whom he gave the job of assigning roles to their people. She remembered what he'd told her when he stayed at her home, explaining his vision for a peaceful tribe.

"It will take the form of the longhouse in which there are many hearths," he'd stated. "One for each family, yet all live as one household under one chief mother. They shall have one mind and live under one law. Thinking will replace killing, and there shall be one commonwealth."

Jigonhsasee gave the men their positions during the gathering to discuss the Great Law of Peace. They were organized into a Great Council, and each of the five tribes was given seats on the Council. The individual tribes would be allowed to elect the leaders that they wanted to send to sit on the Council. The number of seats given to each tribe was based on their size. The Onondaga got 14 seats, the Cayuga got 10, the Oneida got 9, the Mohawk got 9, and the Seneca got 8. She also assigned the women the right to choose the chief of their longhouses, making them a very important part of the Iroquois tribe.

The Iroquois proclaimed Dekanawida the Great Peacemaker for bringing them together. Jigonhsasee was called the Mother of Nations for her role in organizing the Iroquois Confederacy. Hiawatha was honored for turning away from evil to embrace the message of peace and his ability to deliver that message in great speeches. Without these three people, the five tribes would have never stopped fighting. Without the proof that a confederacy with elected leaders working together to solve their problems was a system that could work, the United States of America might not have existed.

Chapter Round-Up Activity

Want to be like the Iroquois and make your own wampum belt? It's pretty easy to create one yourself. All you need are some basic supplies from a craft store. You can come up with your own designs that represent whatever you want. For example, the design of the Hiawatha Belt represents the five tribes of the original Iroquois Confederacy. The middle shape that looks like an arrowhead represents the Onondaga. The two larger squares represent the Cayuga on the left and the Oneida on the right. The smaller square on the left represents the Seneca and the smaller square on the right represents the Mohawk.

Hiawatha's belt.⁶⁶

To make your own wampum belt, you'll need:

- Colored beads
- Scissors
- Tape
- String

Directions:

1. Cut 3 to 5 lengths of string measuring about one foot each.
2. Place the strings on the table horizontally and an equal distance apart.
3. Slide the colored beads onto the strings, making patterns by matching the same colored beads from one string to another.
4. When you've finished with your beads, push the strings together and wrap the tape around the middle and the ends.
5. Show off your wampum belt and tell everyone what the designs represent.

Chapter 6: Inuit Traditions: Stories on Adapting to Arctic Life

The Inuit people are Native Americans living in North America's Arctic and subarctic parts, such as Alaska, Yukon, Northwest Territories, Quebec, Nunavut, Labrador, and Greenland. They have adapted to survive in the extreme cold, using the natural resources around them to build shelter, make clothing, and find food. Since crops can't grow in the freezing climate where they live, the Inuit people are hunters and fishermen. They have also trained dogs to pull sleds to quickly move across the snowy environments. The Inuit people have a rich tradition of stories and legends passed down from generation to generation.

Inuit people.[57]

The Legend of Sedna

Sedna.[58]

Long ago, a fisherman and his wife had a daughter they named Sedna. They lived in a small Inuit village near the freezing sea. Sedna grew up into a beautiful maiden, and Inuit men came from far-off villages to seek her hand in marriage. Many of her suitors were great hunters or fishermen, and they came with gifts they hoped to give Sedna's father in exchange for his blessing to marry her. The hunters brought furs and hides from their most impressive kills, while the fishermen offered the largest fish they could catch. However, Sedna turned every single one of them down, refusing all their marriage proposals.

Her father became upset that she wouldn't take a husband. He argued that she needed to get married and start a family of her own. The more her father pushed her, the more Sedna pushed back, telling him she might never get married. He exploded with anger and demanded that she choose a husband by the next sunrise, or he would kick her out of his home and leave her outside to freeze to death. She had less than a day to find a husband, yet it should have been easy. Every unmarried man in the village was willing to take Sedna as their wife. All she needed to do was go for a walk and pick the first man she saw.

When the sun rose the following morning, Sedna's father went to see whether she'd found herself a husband. Sedna had a big smile on her face and told him that she was married, and he was thrilled to hear this news. His joy immediately turned into rage when Sedna introduced him to her new husband – she had married the lead dog of the family's dog sled team. Fed up with his daughter's disrespect, he grabbed her by the hair and dragged her out of the house. He pulled her down to the shore, threw her into his kayak, and then took the kayak far out to sea.

Once the kayak was far enough that he was sure Sedna wouldn't be able to swim back, he pushed her overboard. She clung to the side of the kayak, begging him to pull her back up, but he grabbed his knife and sliced off her fingers. She fell into the icy waters and sank to the bottom of the sea. Satisfied that he was rid of his troublesome daughter, the fisherman returned home alone.

Instead of drowning as her father intended, Sedna reached the bottom of the sea and was swallowed up by the earth. She tumbled down into the underworld, which the fearsome monsters called home. They were struck by Sedna's beauty and made her their queen, transforming her into a goddess of the sea. When they turned her into a goddess, her fingers that still floated in the sea became seals, walruses, and whales. From that day on, if she became angry, the sea creatures hunted by the Inuits would disappear, so the tribe's shaman had to go out in kayaks and comb her hair to calm her back down. Only then would the sea creatures return.

Anik the Brave

Anik the Brave.[59]

Anik stood near the wall of his family's igloo and watched nervously as his mother pressed her hand to his father's forehead. She turned to Anik with a worried expression and said, "His fever is still very bad. If it does not break soon, he will die."

"Is there anything we can do, mother?" Anik asked.

She shook her head and told him, "I think not, my son. The shaman said that oil from a seal might help him, but this storm is too dangerous for anyone to go out in. The hunters agreed to bring us some seal oil once the storm has passed, but I fear it will be too late by then."

Thinking about his mother's words, Anik decided to kill a seal and bring its oil back for his father. He quietly pulled on his furs to stay warm and grabbed his father's harpoon. While his mother was busy caring for her sick husband, Anik sneaked out of their igloo to brave the storm. As soon as he stepped outside, frost whipped his face, and he struggled to move against the strong winds. Snow pelted him, clinging to his fur clothing, but he forced himself to take one step after another. His progress was slow, but eventually, he made it to the edge of the frozen sea and headed out onto the ice.

The waters were frozen, allowing Anik to walk across the surface, squinting his eyes to see through the haze of the storm. He knew what to look for; holes in the ice the seals used to breathe. It didn't take long for him to find one, but no seals were in sight. Hours passed as Anik waited to glimpse a seal coming to the surface. The wind kept knocking him over, even when he was resting on his knees. He kept having to brush the snow from his clothes, and his face was so numb he could no longer feel it. Anik understood why the hunters refused to go out in this weather. It was miserable.

Anik came close to giving up and returning home empty-handed. His muscles ached from fighting the wind, and his lungs burned from breathing the freezing cold air. Finally, he spotted movement from his half-shut eyes and tightly gripped his father's harpoon. Although he could barely move his arms, he summoned every last ounce of strength he had to thrust the harpoon through the hole in the ice. There was a shrill whine, and the shadow in the water stopped moving. Anik reached into the hole and hauled the dead seal out.

As fast as he could manage, Anik dragged the seal back across the frozen sea, stumbling again and again from the raging winds. He was exhausted by the time he reached his igloo, but he burst inside and called out to his mother.

"I have brought a seal! Come get the oil from it!"

Anik's mother rushed to her son, a combination of fear, anger, and relief showing on her face.

"My son! What have you done? Did you go out in this storm?"

"Yes, mother," he said. "I could not sit by and do nothing while father suffered. Now you can save him."

She pushed his hood down and kissed the top of his head, saying, "You brave, foolish boy! You could have died out there!"

"But I did not," he replied. "Do not worry about me. Do what you need to help father."

His mother hurried to extract the seal's oil and gave it to her husband. She also cut its meat and made a broth for him to eat, as the shaman had told her the seal had great healing powers. Anik was sound asleep, but when he awoke, he also found some meat and broth waiting for him. His mother insisted he eat it to help him recover from his difficult adventure. He did as she asked, but he was still exhausted and fell back asleep when he had finished.

Anik woke up again the next morning and opened his eyes, looking over at where his father had been resting. There was nobody there and, for a moment, he was terrified that his father had died. However, he felt a hand pat his cheek and looked up to see his father smiling down at him.

"I heard what you did to save my life," his father said. "You are braver than every man in this village. I will never forget how you braved the storm and hunted a seal to help me. You will be a great leader when you are grown, and I will be the first to follow you."

His father was right. Anik became the best hunter in the village, and he became known for his bravery. He earned a reputation for achieving incredible feats, helping save many lives, and keeping the village safe. Eventually, the old chief died without any children to take his place. The villagers got together to pick a new chief, and Anik's father was the first to put forward his son's name. After everything Anik had done for them, the decision was easy, and he was chosen to replace the old chief. Anik's father stayed true to his word, serving as his son's top advisor and loyally following his new chief.

Chapter Round-Up Activity

When you read these Inuit tales, could you picture the scenes and characters in your mind?

Take some time to draw your own version of something you really liked from the stories in this chapter. It can be anything you want; a picture of Sedna, an igloo, a seal, a dog sled, or whatever else you want to draw. You can draw your picture on the next page, or if you're using an e-reader or reading in an e-book format, you can draw your picture in a notebook or drawing pad.

My Picture from the Inuit Tales

Chapter 7: Apache Spirituality: The Sacred Hoop and Life's Journey

The Apache people are Native Americans from multiple tribes that originally lived in the Great Plains Southwest of the United States and the northern part of Mexico. They fought many wars against the Spanish Conquistadors, the Mexican people, and the United States Army. The Apache are a fierce and proud people who resisted attempts to push them out of their lands. From 1875 to 1886, the United States forcibly removed the Apache from their homes and resettled them on reservations in Oklahoma, New Mexico, and Arizona.

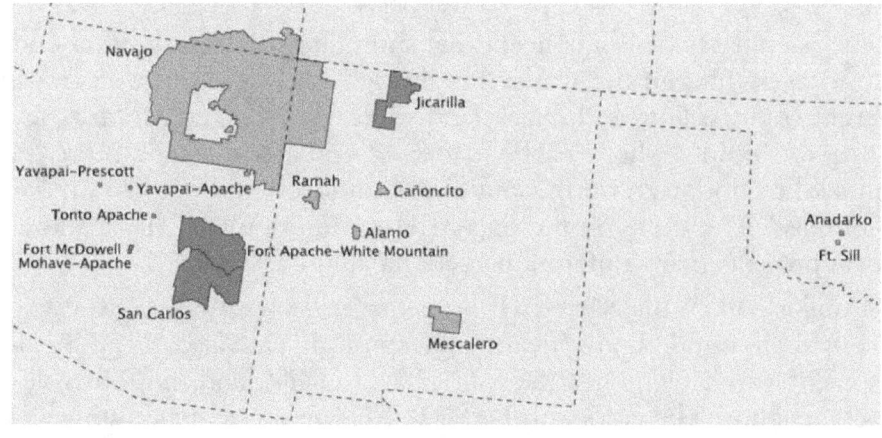

Apachean present.[60]

The Sacred Hoop

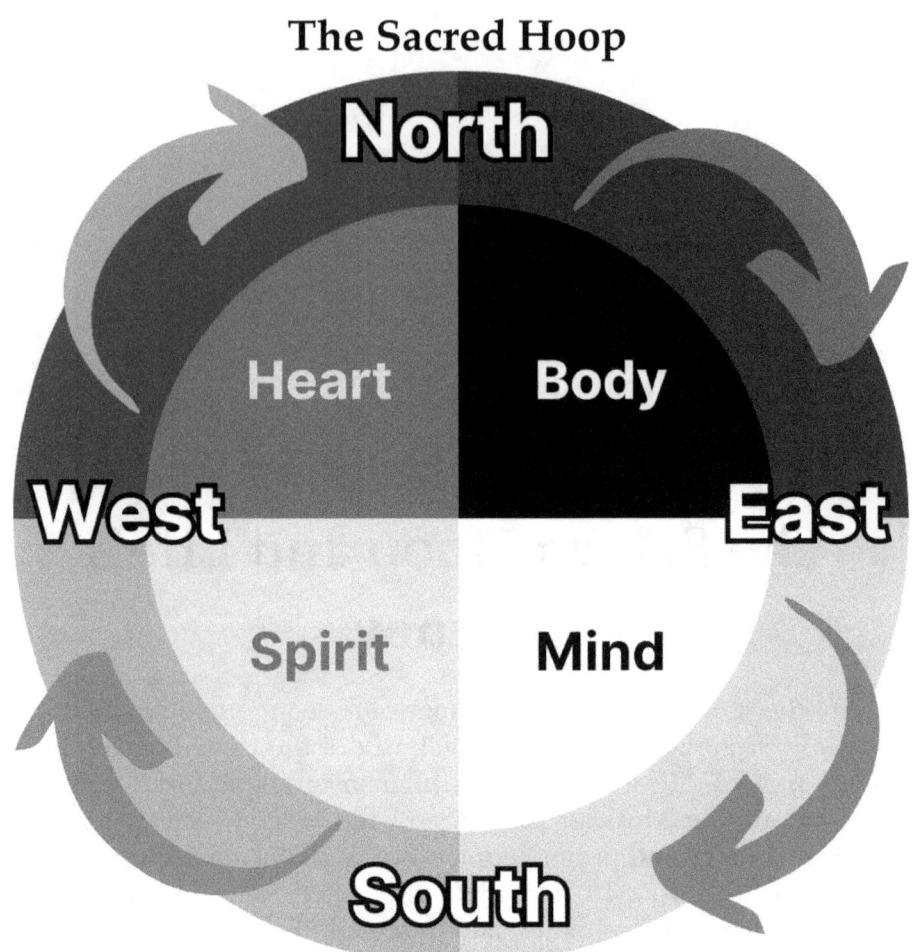

The Sacred Hoop.

The Sacred Hoop is a concept that shows how there is a never-ending cycle to everything in the world. It's divided into four parts, each with a different color: yellow, red, black, and white. The Sacred Hoop is set up so that the points where each quarter of the hoop meets represent a cardinal direction, with north, south, east, and west laid out like on a map or compass. The cycle on the Sacred Hoop flows to the right, and each color represents many different parts of life and the world.

A major part of the Sacred Hoop is that it shows the four aspects of a person: their mind, body, heart, and spirit. It can also show the four seasons, the four elements, the four phases of life, and the four roles of Apache culture. The colors of the Sacred Hoop are matched up with the following parts of each group:

- **Yellow:** Represents the Spirit and a person's willpower, Spring, Fire, Birth/Rebirth, The Visionary.
- **Red:** Represents the Heart and a person's emotions, Summer, Water, Growth, and The Teacher.
- **Black:** Represents the Body and a person's physical form, Autumn, Earth, Maturity, The Healer.
- **White:** Represents the Mind and a person's intellect, Winter, Air, Death, The Warrior.

Apache Creation Myth

At the start of the universe, there was nothing but darkness. Out of nowhere, a small, thin disc appeared. The top side was colored yellow, and the bottom side was colored black. In the middle of the disc was a tiny man – no bigger than a frog – who had a long white beard. His name was Kuterastan, and he was the first god to come into being. When he awakened, he rubbed his eyes and opened them. Looking up into the darkness, he saw a bright light appear. The light shone down on the darkness below.

Kuterastan looked to the east, and the light took on the yellow color of dawn. He looked west, and the light became an amber color like dusk. He searched around him and saw clouds that weren't there before. After rubbing his eyes and face, he shook the sweat from his hands, flinging it away. Another cloud appeared, but this one had a small girl sitting atop it. Her name was Stenatliha – or the "woman without parents." As Kuterastan and Stenatliha looked at each other, they seemed confused.

"Where did you come from?" Kuterastan asked.

"I do not know," Stenatliha answered. "Where did *you* come from?"

"I do not know, either," he replied.

She thought for a moment and then said, "You should come join me on my cloud."

He climbed off the disc and sat down beside her. Once again, he rubbed his eyes and face, shaking his hands and flinging sweat everywhere. The sweat transformed into Chuganaai, or the Sun, and Hadintin Skhin, or Pollen Boy. For a long time, all four of the gods sat on the cloud in complete silence. None of them knew what to say or do.

It was Kuterastan who spoke first, asking, "What shall we do?"

"We could create something," Stenatliha suggested.

Pollen Boy frowned and said, "But what should we create?"

"It does not matter," Chuganaai insisted. "Just make the first thing that comes to mind."

So Kuterastan flicked his sweat and made Nacholecho, the Tarantula. He followed this up by creating the Big Dipper, the Wind, the Lightning, the Thunder, and the Moon. The gods assigned each a task. However, as they sat on the cloud, they agreed that it wasn't a very good home. All four gods dripped beads of sweat into Kuterastan's hands. He closed his palms, and when he opened them again, there was a little brown ball the size of a bean. The four gods kicked the ball back and forth, causing it to grow each time.

The Wind entered the ball and caused it to get even bigger. Nacholecho attached a black cord to the ball and stretched it out far to the east. He then attached a white cord and stretched it to the south, a yellow cord that stretched to the east, and a red cord that stretched to the north. Finally, the gods stuck poles into each cord to hold it in place.

"The world is now made, and it sits still," Kuterastan said and repeated this phrase over and over.

Kuterastan, Stenatliha, and Pollen Boy entered the world to live there. However, Chuganaai chose to remain in the skies above, having fallen in love with the Moon. She did not return his feelings, but he continues to chase her around the world each day, never able to catch up to her. The other three gods used their sweat to form the oceans, mountains, plants, and animals. Finally, Kuterastan and Stenatliha combined their sweat and created the first humans, teaching them all about their new world.

Hauzini's Sunrise Dance Ceremony

Hanuzi's sunrise dance ceremony statue.[61]

The time had arrived for Hauzini's coming-of-age ceremony, which all Apache girls must go through: the Sunrise Dance Ceremony. She wasn't looking forward to it, dreading the fact that she would be spending the next four days doing nothing but dancing in place. She didn't understand why it was so important. Nothing would change just because she bounced around for four days in a row. She begged her mother to let her skip it, but her mother was outraged that she would even ask. It seemed that there was no way for her to get out of participating in the ceremony.

A blanket was set out a little way from their village for Hauzini to stand on and perform the dance. At sundown, the ceremony began. The tribe's medicine man started the ceremony with a blessing, and then she was told to stand on the blanket. Her mother dressed her in buckskins, scarves, beads, shells, and sacred yellow pollen. She was given a curved staff that was to be used to keep in rhythm with the music being played. The last part of her outfit was a large eagle feather placed in her hair. As the drums beat, she danced by shifting her weight from one foot to the other throughout each traditional song.

On the first night, 32 songs were played by the medicine man and a group of chosen singers. Hauzini was tired by the time they were finished and was glad to go to her meditation teepee, which was built specifically for the ceremony. It was set up close to where she danced, and she was meant to spend the night in prayer. She had to fast throughout the ceremony, only being given water to drink. As she meditated and prayed, an owl flew down from the sky and landed in front of her. She stared at it and wondered why it had come. When it opened its beak, instead of hearing a hoot, it actually spoke to her.

"Hello, Changing Woman," the owl said. "I have come to pay my respects."

"I am Hauzini, not the Changing Woman," she replied.

The owl laughed and told her, "I have known you since the beginning, Changing Woman. You cannot fool me."

The owl then flew away, leaving Hauzini confused. At sunrise, she returned to the blanket to dance again. It was hot and humid, which left her uncomfortable dressed in her outfit. After six hours of dancing, people from the village and beyond came to offer her blessings. Others came to be blessed by her because they believed the sacred yellow pollen gave her special healing powers. She touched them and spoke the traditional prayers of healing, and they thanked her, calling her Changing Woman, just like the owl had.

Her tribe feasted that evening, having acorn stew, barbecue corn, beans, and cornbread. She smelled the food and felt her stomach rumbling with hunger, but all she could have was more water. The Crown Dancers arrived and danced with bells to 32 songs. Hauzini danced with them, and they offered blessings from the spirits to her. At midnight, the Crown Dancers finished and left, followed by the rest of the tribe. However, Hauzini had to dance all through the night to the beat of the medicine man's drums.

During the night, a coyote stalked toward her from the darkness. She looked at it fearfully and called out a warning to the medicine man, but he didn't seem to hear her. Hauzini was about to stop dancing so she could run away, but the coyote opened its mouth and spoke.

"Do not be afraid, Changing Woman. I have only come to pay my respects."

"Thank you, Coyote," Hauzini said.

The coyote turned and walked away. Inside, Hauzini began to feel different. Her muscles stopped aching, and her bones felt stronger. By the morning, all weariness had melted away from her body. The sun climbed into the sky, and she stopped dancing so she could mash corn and clay together so the tribe could paint her yellow from head to toe. Another 32 songs were played for the now-painted Hauzini to dance along with. The Crown Dancers returned to join her one more time. Her tribe built an altar in her teepee, laying out sacred feathers on it and offering prayers.

Hauzini continued to dance alone all night, and instead of feeling tired, she felt the power of her ancestors flowing through her. When a bear appeared before her, she smiled at it and greeted it first.

"Hello, my old friend," she said. "It is good to see you again."

"It is good to see you, too, Changing Woman," the bear replied. "I wished to come pay my respects."

"Thank you, old friend," Hauzini replied gratefully. "I appreciate your thoughtfulness."

When the sun rose that morning, her tribe returned to finish the ceremony. Her mother took her down to the river to wash her. The medicine man gave a final blessing and released Hauzini. After carefully removing each item of her outfit, she was allowed to go home and sleep. Now that it was over, she felt exhausted and was happy for the chance to rest. When she awoke the next day, having slept for almost 24 hours, she no longer felt like a girl – she was a changed woman.

Chapter 8: The Hopi and the Corn Mother: Tales of Agriculture and Survival

The Hopi people are Native Americans living in the Southwestern United States, mainly in northeastern Arizona. They have a lot in common with the Navajo and the Pueblo peoples, such as living in homes made from adobe and honoring kachina spirits. The Hopi have a female-based culture, with families centered on the women. Children are considered part of their mother's clan, while the women of the father's clan get to name them. The Hopi people are subsistence farmers, so they only grow enough food to feed themselves and their families or communities.

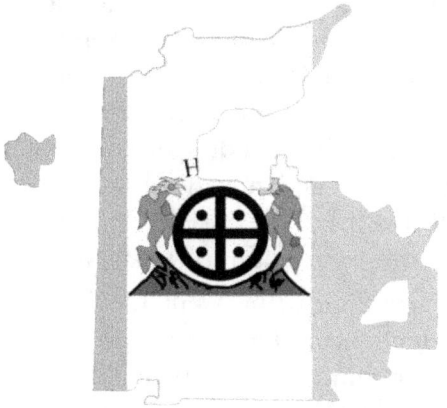

Map of the Hopi Reservation[62]

The Corn Mother

Traditional Hopi Woman.[68]

Many ages before today, food in the lands of the Hopi was hard to come by. Not far from a starving tribe lived an old woman known as the Corn Mother. War or starvation caused children to become orphans, and one of the orphans wandered away from his village, ending up at the Corn Mother's home. Taking pity on the child, she took him into her home. He, too, was starving, and she couldn't bear to watch the boy suffer. In secret, she rubbed her body and produced grains of corn for him to eat. When he returned to his tribe, they couldn't understand how he seemed well-fed while they themselves continued to starve.

One day, a man from the tribe went to visit the Corn Mother. He begged her to help feed his tribe by whatever means she had fed the orphan. She took pity on him, just like the child, and agreed to bring them food. Again, she rubbed her body, filling a large basket with grains of corn. When she brought the food to the tribe, they were overjoyed and finally filled their starving bellies. The tribe's chief thanked the Corn Mother for her generosity and invited her to join them. They gave her a house in the village, and she was happy to be accepted by the people.

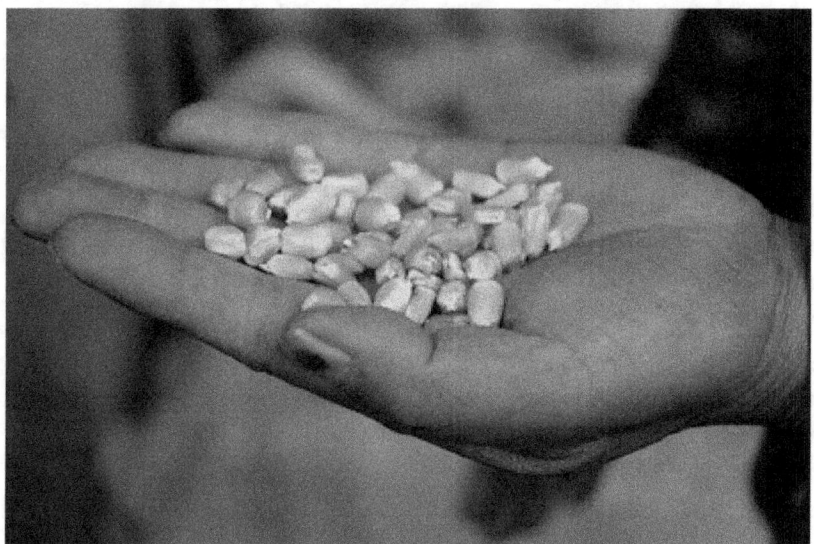

The Corn Mother fed the tribe with the corn she made from her body."

The Corn Mother kept the tribe fed for several years but became weaker every time she made corn from her body. The tribe depended on her to survive, and she feared the time would come when she could no longer feed them. During an unusually cold winter, the tribe once again had no food. Making the corn for everyone took a toll on the Corn Mother, and she became too weak to stand. The chief went to her home, where he found her lying in bed and begged her to give them more food. Since she could not get out of bed to make the corn in secret, she first refused, but the chief pleaded with her on behalf of the starving children.

She took pity on the tribe and told the chief to bring her a basket. When he carried it to her, she rubbed her body to create the grains of corn for them to eat. However, seeing how their food had been made disgusted the chief. He called her a witch and spread the word to the tribe. They decided to burn her for using evil magic to make the corn. Before she was burned, the orphan she first helped tried to convince the tribe not to kill her. They ignored his pleas, but the Corn Mother was grateful to him for trying.

The orphan hugged the Corn Mother with tears, apologizing for failing to help her the way she helped him. She told him not to cry and instructed him to bury her bones in a field after she was dead. The tribe dragged the

Corn Mother far from their village and set her on fire, leaving her to burn to death. They then returned to their homes, but the orphan stayed behind, begging the spirits to prevent the Corn Mother from suffering and asking them to take care of her when she joined them.

After the flames died out, the orphan collected her bones and found an empty field in which to bury her bones. He returned to his village, saddened at the loss of the kind old woman who saved him and his tribe. Every day, the orphan went to the Corn Mother's grave to offer a blessing and honor her sacrifice. He noticed that plants were starting to sprout all across the field. Great big stalks rose up throughout the summer, each one holding husks of corn. By the end of the summer, huge ears of corn were ripe to be picked.

Despite their poor treatment of the Corn Mother, she had provided the tribe with a way to keep the starving people fed. They ate the corn, but the orphan saved some to remove the kernels and plant them in the field. In this way, the tribe was able to grow corn crops every year and feed themselves well. The gift given to them by the Corn Mother was shared with others in the area, allowing them all to survive. When the orphan grew up and had a family of his own, he made sure to pass on the story of the Corn Mother to his children. Many years later, he died with a full belly and a loving family surrounding him, and his spirit was finally reunited with the Corn Mother.

Chapter Round-Up Activity

Do you like to eat corn? Have you ever seen a cornfield? Would you like to watch it grow? You can plant your own corn to see how it goes from a seed to a cornstalk that produces big ears of corn. All you have to do is follow these instructions to make your own corn to pick and enjoy:

What You Need:

- A plant pot
- Potting mix soil
- Fertilizer
- Watering can
- Corn seeds (kernels)

Directions:

1. Fill the pot with your potting mix soil until it's about 2 inches from the top.
2. Dig a small hole in the center of the soil about 1 to 2 inches deep.
3. Drop in your corn seeds and cover them back up with the soil.
4. Use the watering can to pour plenty of water into the pot.
5. Spread some fertilizer over the soil.
6. Place the pot in a spot where it can get 6 to 8 hours of sunlight daily.
7. Make sure you keep the soil moist and use the fertilizer on it once every 14 days.
8. Within two to three months, you will have your own corn!

Chapter 9: Tlingit Totems: Carving Histories and Clan Legends

The Tlingit people are Native Americans who live in Alaska and the Pacific Northwest Coast of the United States. They have a system of kinship or family structure based on the female line. As with the Hopi, children are considered part of their mother's clan, and roles and property are passed down from mother to daughter. A big part of Tlingit life revolves around catching and eating salmon, but they also hunt land and sea mammals.

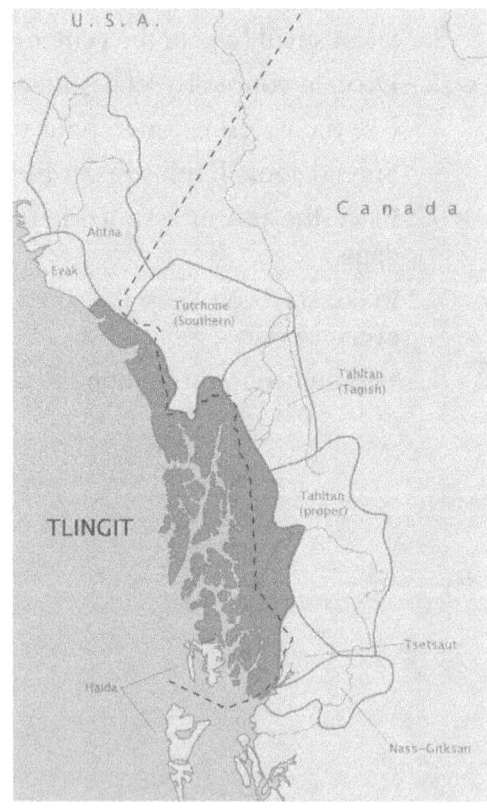

The map of Tinglit.[65]

Totem Poles

One major aspect of Tlingit culture is the carefully crafted and highly detailed totem poles they create. These totem poles are usually made from cedar trees, and the figures they carve tell a story. Many totem poles use animals to represent different ideas, traditions, or folktales, allowing them to express their own unique version of events for people to see. Observers need to be familiar with the legends and mythology of Tlingit culture to understand what the totem poles mean.

A Tlinglit totem pole.[66]

Types of Totem Poles

Lineage Pole (Entrance Pole): These are often used as support rafters on the inside and outside of houses. They show a family's history and social status within their tribe.

Native Legend and Story Pole: These display figures to represent the legends and stories passed down through the generations of the tribe.

Memorial Pole: These are carved to honor the lives of important elders and tribe members, especially those who have done great deeds or aided the tribe in some way.

Commemorative Pole: These are made to mark major celebrations, festivals, feasts, and other special events.

Grave Marker Pole: These are carved with figures to represent the lives of dead tribe members. They are hollowed out in order to hold the remains of the dead.

Common Totem Pole Figures

The Thunderbird is a common totem.[67]

Raven: The Raven is a major figure in many Tlingit legends. He is a trickster spirit who uses his wits and intelligence to defeat greedy or evil individuals and help the good people they hurt. There are groups of Tlingit clans who use the Raven as their symbol.

Thunderbird: The Thunderbird is believed to flap its wings and create the thunder heard during thunderstorms. One legend tells of how the Thunderbird helped the Tlingit when the Whale ate all the sea fish. The Thunderbird used its mighty wings to battle the Whale, defeating it and allowing the Tlingit to catch fish once again.

Eagle: The Eagle represents the wind and the skies. It is considered a sacred animal, and its feathers are said to hold great power. Like the Raven, groups of clans have taken the Eagle as their symbol.

Otter: The Otter is another major figure in Tlingit mythology. A group of helpful shapeshifting spirits known as the *Kushtaka* often appear in the form of the Otter. They can also transform into a half-human and half-otter being. The Kushtaka aid the Tlingit by giving them food and guidance.

Wolf: The Wolf is one of the few land animals that appear in Tlingit legends. It represents a combination of danger, strength, and hunting skills. As with the Raven and the Eagle, groups of clans use the Wolf as their symbol.

The Raven and the Box of Light

The Raven.

A man called Nass Shaak Aankáawu, or the "Nobleman at the Head of the Nass River," was greedy. He collected many treasures, keeping them all to himself. His most precious treasures were every form of light, which he kept in boxes stored in his home. This left the world covered in never-ending darkness. The people begged Nass Shaak Aankáawu to return the light so they could have a day and a night, but he refused. He didn't want to share his treasures with anyone else because he believed he deserved to have everything he desired.

There was a trickster spirit in the form of a white Raven named Yéil who wanted to know what it was like to be human. While watching the Tlingit people, he saw Nass Shaak Aankáawu's daughter go down to a stream and drink its water every morning. Yéil transformed into a needle from a spruce tree and jumped into the stream. He floated into her cup, and she swallowed him when she drank from it. The woman became pregnant and gave birth to Yéil in human form. Nass Shaak Aankáawu and his daughter adored the child, loving him more than anything else in their lives.

Nass Shaak Aankáawu spoiled his grandson, giving him every toy and luxury the boy could ever want. When the child cried that he wanted the boxes holding the stars, the moon, and the sun, his grandfather could not say no to him. Every time baby Yéil cried for one of the treasures, Nass Shaak Aankáawu gave it to him. As soon as Yéil got the boxes, he opened them up, releasing the stars, the moon, and the sun, returning the light to the world. Nass Shaak Aankáawu was upset at losing his treasures, but the people and animals were delighted to have them back.

Realizing he had been tricked, Nass Shaak Aankáawu wanted revenge for losing his treasures. He grabbed Yéil and held him over the fireplace, letting him become marked by the smoke. Yéil's human form melted away, and he was once again in the shape of a Raven. The smoke changed his coloring from white to black; from that day on, every raven would be born with feathers the color of coal. The Tlingit people honored Yéil by carving the Raven at the top of their totem poles, thanking him for returning the light to them.

Chapter Round-Up Activity

Do you have a story you want to tell? Maybe there's someone important in your life you want to honor. You can create a totem pole to express whatever you want. To make one yourself, here's what you need to do:

What You Need:

- Drawing paper
- Paper towel tube
- Crayons or markers
- Scissors
- Tape
- Ruler

Directions:

1. Use the crayons or markers to draw figures of animals or symbols. Make 3 or 4 figures about 3 inches tall and 2 to 3 inches wide. Measure your drawings with the ruler to make sure they're the right size.

2. Cut out the figures you drew with the scissors.

3. Make a loop with the tape so the sticky side is on the outside and stick it to the back of each cutout figure.

4. Attach the cutout figures with the tape to the paper towel tube. Place them one on top of the other, making them look like a totem pole. The tube is 11 inches tall, so they should all fit if you measured your figures correctly. Part of the top figure can be a bit above the top of the tube.

Display your totem pole where people can see it. Explain to them the story you've created and what each figure represents.

Conclusion

It's good to get into the habit of expanding your mind by learning new things. There are people worldwide who live in a way completely different from your own. When you take the time to explore their history and culture, you will find that there's more than one way to do things. Some people have ideas, traditions, and beliefs that aren't the same as yours, but it doesn't mean you can't understand why they live the way they do.

The Native Americans have done their best to keep their culture and spirit alive. Being pushed out of their homelands and onto reservations also came with the United States trying to make them change. There have been many attempts to force the Native American tribes into becoming more like the people of the United States, as well as trying to convert them from their traditional religions to Christianity. This has left the Native Americans struggling to balance their original culture with the culture of the rest of the country.

Now that you've learned many new things about the different Native American tribes, you can help them keep their culture alive. Spread these tales by telling them to your family and friends. Show them the projects you've made that are based on Native American arts and crafts. Talk about the facts you discovered – since many people never learned them in school. Think about everything you read and how you can use the lessons taught by these Native American stories in your own daily life.

Check out another book in the series

Welcome Aboard, Check Out This Limited-Time Free Bonus!

Ahoy, reader! Welcome to the Ahoy Publications family, and thanks for snagging a copy of this book! Since you've chosen to join us on this journey, we'd like to offer you something special.

Check out the link below for a FREE e-book filled with delightful facts about American History.

But that's not all - you'll also have access to our exclusive email list with even more free e-books and insider knowledge. Well, what are ye waiting for? Click the link below to join and set sail toward exciting adventures in American History.

Access your bonus here
https://ahoypublications.com/
Or, Scan the QR code!

References

Part 1: Inspiring Native American Stories for Kids

Aktá Lakota Museum & Cultural Center. (n.d.). The Legend of the White Buffalo Woman. Aktá Lakota Museum & Cultural Center. https://aktalakota.stjo.org/lakota-legends/white-buffalo-woman/

Americans, N. (n.d.). Biography: Sitting Bull | American Experience | PBS. Www.pbs.org. https://www.pbs.org/wgbh/americanexperience/features/oakley-sitting-bull/

Araminta, M. (2023, May 23). The Geography of Mi'kmaq Folklore. ArcGIS StoryMaps. https://storymaps.arcgis.com/stories/b0fca956f299408ba4b8c2e3d4a47995

Azure, L. B. (2016, February 22). Actualizing the Seventh Generation Prophecy: A Case Study in Teacher Education at a Tribal College. Tribal College Journal of American Indian Higher Education. https://tribalcollegejournal.org/actualizing-the-seventh-generation-prophecy-a-case-study-in-teacher-education-at-a-tribal-college

Bob, B. (2021). CHIEF SEATTLE'S LETTER. Csun.edu. https://www.csun.edu/~vcpsy00h/seattle.htm

Brando, E. (2010). Wilma Mankiller. National Women's History Museum. https://www.womenshistory.org/education-resources/biographies/wilma-mankiller

Brown, J. (2020, October 23). What Is the Story of Glooscap? – KnowledgeBurrow.com. Knowledgeburrow.com. https://knowledgeburrow.com/what-is-the-story-of-glooscap/

Caduto, M. J., & Bruchac, J. (1998). Keepers of Life: Discovering Plants through Native American Stories and Earth Activities for Children. Fulcrum Pub.

CBC. (2020, March 4). Who is Glooscap? He's kind, respectful, and big, says Mi'kmaw educator. CBC. https://www.cbc.ca/news/canada/nova-scotia/legend-of-glooscap-mi-kmaw-culture-columnist-trevor-sanipass-1.5484002

Christo, C. (2021, August 4). The Hopi Prophecies Are Coming True — Here's Why We Should Pay Attention. The Hill; The Hill. https://thehill.com/changing-america/opinion/566362-the-hopi-prophecies-are-coming-true-heres-why-we-should-pay

DeGuzman, K. (2020, September 12). What is a Fable — Definition, Examples & Characteristics. StudioBinder. https://www.studiobinder.com/blog/what-is-a-fable-definition/

Goble, P. (1998). The Lost Children: The Boys Who Were Neglected. Simon & Schuster Children's Publishing Division.

History.com Editors. (2009, November 16). Chief Seattle Dies Near the City Named for Him. HISTORY. https://www.history.com/this-day-in-history/chief-seattle-dies-near-the-city-named-for-him

History.com Editors. (2009, November 9). Sitting Bull. HISTORY; A&E Television Networks. https://www.history.com/topics/native-american-history/sitting-bull

Institute for Public Relations. (2021, October 22). Native American Pioneer Chief Seattle (c. 1786 – 1866) | Institute for Public Relations. Instituteforpr.org. https://instituteforpr.org/native-american-pioneer-chief-seattle/

Jo, M. (2020, August 12). Learn More about the Legend of Chief Seattle - Discovering Washington State. Discovering Washington State. https://www.discoveringwashingtonstate.com/learn-more-about-the-legend-of-chief-seattle/

Judson L., M. (2004, April 28). The Raven in Native American Mythology. Judson L Moore. https://www.judsonlmoore.com/the-raven-in-native-american-mythology

Judson, K. (2004, October 9). Native American Stories (Myth-Folklore Online). Mythfolklore.net. https://www.mythfolklore.net/3043mythfolklore/reading/california/pages/06.htm

Keim, F. (n.d.). Marshall Cultural Atlas. Www.ankn.uaf.edu. http://www.ankn.uaf.edu/NPE/CulturalAtlases/Yupiaq/Marshall/raven/RavenStealsTheLight.html

Mall, L. (2018, February 12). Greatest Lakota Leaders Who Ever Lived – Lakota Mall. Lakota Mall. https://www.lakotamall.com/greatest-lakota-leaders/

Mark, J. J. (2023, November 20). Falling Star. World History Encyclopedia. https://www.worldhistory.org/article/2329/falling-star

Mark, J. J. (2024, January 19). Cheyenne Legends of the Buffalo. World History Encyclopedia. https://www.worldhistory.org/article/2353/cheyenne-legends-of-the-buffalo/

Matthews, A. S. (2022, February 2). Spirituality and Religious Beliefs of the Mi'kmaq. ArcGIS StoryMaps. https://storymaps.arcgis.com/stories/ee889ed588034218a63ce56971ebf820

McLeod, T. (2017). Hopi Prophecy—A Timeless Warning. Sacred Land. https://sacredland.org/hopi-prophecy

Millman, L. (1987). A Kayak Full of Ghosts. Capra Press.Native American Mythology. (2024). Twinkl.co.za. https://www.twinkl.co.za/teaching-wiki/native-american-mythology

Nair, N. (2022, October 5). Saquasohuh : The Blue Star Kachina. Mythlok. https://mythlok.com/saquasohuh

National Park Service. (2016). Sitting Bull - Little Bighorn Battlefield National Monument (U.S. National Park Service). Nps.gov. https://www.nps.gov/libi/learn/historyculture/sitting-bull.htm

Nordquist, R. (2019, May 4). Which of Your Favorite Stories are Actually Fables? ThoughtCo. https://www.thoughtco.com/what-is-a-fable-1690848

Pastore, R. T. (2016, October). Traditional Mi'kmaq (Micmac) Culture. Www.heritage.nf.ca. https://www.heritage.nf.ca/articles/indigenous/mikmaq-culture.php

Plains Indians - Cheyenne - Native Americans in Olden Times for Kids. (2019). Mrdonn.org. https://nativeamericans.mrdonn.org/plains/cheyenne.html

Ramirez, S. (2022, June 6). Wilma Mankiller Led as the First Woman Principal Chief of the Cherokee Nation. Smithsonian American Women's History. https://womenshistory.si.edu/blog/wilma-mankiller-led-first-woman-principal-chief-cherokee-nation

Reading Rockets. (n.d.). Native American Traditional Tales and Legends | Reading Rockets. Www.readingrockets.org. https://www.readingrockets.org/books-and-authors/booklists/american-indian-and-alaska-native-history-and-culture/native-american

Reed, J. (2024, March 13). The Life of Wilma Mankiller, First Woman to Serve as Principal Chief of the Cherokee Nation | National Trust for Historic Preservation. Savingplaces.org. https://savingplaces.org/guides/wilma-mankiller-first-woman-principal-chief-cherokee-nation

Sitting Bull (Tatanka Yotanka). (2017, August 2). UNHCR Central Europe. https://www.unhcr.org/ceu/9507-sitting-bull-tatanka-yotanka.html

Smith, S. (2015, September 16). The Legend of the Whispering Wind. Motherhood in Technicolor. https://www.motherhoodintechnicolor.com/the-legend-of-the-whispering-wind/

Stekel, P. (n.d.). Chief Seattle. HistoryNet. https://www.historynet.com/chief-seattle/

Summer, B. (2014, November 30). PPT - Mi'kmaq Creation Stories PowerPoint Presentation, free download - ID:7047989. SlideServe. https://www.slideserve.com/summer-barr/mi-kmaq-creation-stories

The Admin. (2024, February 24). Native American Tales: Unveiling Legends and Their Meanings. SOCIALSTUDIESHELP.COM. https://socialstudieshelp.com/native-american-tales-unveiling-legends-and-their-meanings/

The Hopi Origin Story | Native America. (n.d.). PBS LearningMedia. https://www.pbslearningmedia.org/resource/hopi-origin-story/hopi-origin-story/

Tribal Directory. (2016). Tlingit Raven Story. Tribaldirectory.com. https://tribaldirectory.com/information/tlingit-raven.html

Welker, G. (n.d.). How the Buffalo Hunt Began. Indians.org. https://indians.org/welker/buffhunt.htm

What is Folklore? – Social Sciences, Health, and Education Library (SSHEL) – U of I Library. (2019). Illinois.edu. https://www.library.illinois.edu/sshel/specialcollections/folklore/definition/

Wilson, L. (n.d.). Mankiller, Wilma Pearl | The Encyclopedia of Oklahoma History and Culture. Www.okhistory.org. https://www.okhistory.org/publications/enc/entry.php?entry=MA013

Part 2: Empowering Native American Stories For Children

Access Genealogy. (2011, July 9). Blackfoot Tribe | Access Genealogy. Access Genealogy. http://www.accessgenealogy.com/native/tribes/siouan/blackfoothist.htm

All Tribes. (2019). Types of Native American Kachina Dolls. Alltribes.com. https://alltribes.com/types-of-native-american-kachina-dolls/

Arizona Museum of Natural History. (2020, October 22). Apache Sunrise Dance and Ceremony | Arizona Museum of Natural History. Www.arizonamuseumofnaturalhistory.org. https://www.arizonamuseumofnaturalhistory.org/explore-the-museum/exhibitions/athapascan-way/apache-sunrise-dance-and-ceremony#ad-image-0

Associated Press. (1962, March 25). Article on Bob Barker 1962. Argus-Leader, 17. https://www.newspapers.com/article/argus-leader-article-on-bob-barker-1962/93129234/

Belarde-Lewis, M. (2019, July 21). There are many versions of the Tlingit "Raven" story, but its truth and hopeful message are universal. The Seattle Times. https://www.seattletimes.com/pacific-nw-magazine/there-are-many-versions-of-the-tlingit-raven-story-but-its-truth-and-hopeful-message-are-universal/

Borré, K. (1994). The Healing Power of the Seal: The Meaning of Intuit Health Practice and Belief. Arctic Anthropology, 31(1), 1–15. https://www.jstor.org/stable/40316345

Brummett, Jr., R. (1982). The Tribes and the States. Www.sidis.net. https://www.sidis.net/TSContents.htm

Corn Mothers. (2016). Corn Mothers | Home. Www.cornmothers.com. https://www.cornmothers.com/

Drexler, K. (2019, January 22). Research Guides: Indian Removal Act: Primary Documents in American History: Introduction. Loc.gov; Library of Congress. https://guides.loc.gov/indian-removal-act

Farrand, T. (2022, August 3). Corn Mother: Mythical origins of the world's most produced crop. Www.artsundivided.com. https://www.artsundivided.com/post/2022-08-03-corn-mother

Goseyun, A. E. (2023). Balch Institute—Rites of Passage—Sunrise Ceremonial. Hsp.org. https://www2.hsp.org/exhibits/Balch%20exhibits/rites/apache.html

Grossnickle Hines, A. (2016, March 4). Peaceful Pieces. Web.archive.org. https://web.archive.org/web/20160304033735/http://www.aghines.com/anna_html_pages/peaceful/peacemaker.htm

Johnson, E. (2019). Sutori. Www.sutori.com. https://www.sutori.com/en/story/dekanawida-the-great-peacemaker--XGmBGZdZKqmxjVz5kjEEPjpE

Kachina House. (2021, March 23). 10 Navajo Symbols and Their Meanings. Kachina House's Blog. https://blog.kachinahouse.com/10-important-navajo-symbols-and-their-meanings/

Klein, C. (2019, November 7). How Native Americans Struggled to Survive on the Trail of Tears. History.com. https://www.history.com/news/trail-of-tears-conditions-cherokee

Kudu, R. (2016, October 16). Rain Dance of Zuni. Www.inquiry.net. http://www.inquiry.net/outdoor/native/dance/rain_zuni.htm

Library of Congress. (2011). New Mexico. The Rain Dance. Zuni Pueblo. Library of Congress, Washington, D.C. 20540 USA. https://www.loc.gov/item/2017657465/

Mescalero Apache Tribe. (2019). Our Culture. Mescaleroapachetribe.com. https://mescaleroapachetribe.com/our-culture/

Minges, P. (1994). Beneath the Underdog: Race, Religion and the Trail of Tears. Cherokee, Native American. U.S. Data Repository, USGenNet Inc. Www.us-Data.org. https://www.us-data.org/us/minges/underdog.html

National Park Service. (2016). Bison Bellows: Indigenous Hunting Practices (U.S. National Park Service). Nps.gov. https://www.nps.gov/articles/bison-bellows-3-31-16.htm

Native Languages. (1998). Native Lore: Apache Creation Story. Www.ilhawaii.net. http://www.ilhawaii.net/~stony/lore34.html

Parker, A. C. (1916). ᴧ/ork State Museum Bullet iUl. https://ia801604.us.archive.org/19/items/constitutionoffi00parkuoft/constitutionoffi00parkuoft.pdf

Pembroke, H. (2021, May 21). The History and Significance of Totem Poles. Alaska Wildlife Alliance (AWA). https://www.akwildlife.org/news/the-history-and-significance-of-totem-poles

Roediger, V. M. (1991). Ceremonial Costumes of the Pueblo Indians. Publishing.cdlib.org. https://publishing.cdlib.org/ucpressebooks/view?docId=ft8870087s&chunk.id=d0e1214&toc.depth=1&toc.id=d0e950&brand=ucpress

Severo, R. (2023, August 26). Bob Barker, Longtime Host of "The Price Is Right," Dies at 99. The New York Times. https://www.nytimes.com/2023/08/26/arts/television/bob-barker-dead.html

Soulek, L. (2024, January 12). Native American Treaty Law 101. KELOLAND.com. https://www.keloland.com/news/local-news/native-american-treaty-law-101/

Weiser-Alexander, K. (2018, October). The Thunderbird of Native Americans – Legends of America. Www.legendsofamerica.com. https://www.legendsofamerica.com/thunderbird-native-american/

Image Sources

1 https://pixabay.com/illustrations/fantasy-unicorn-rainbow-pegasus-7457387/

2 https://commons.wikimedia.org/wiki/File:Le_G%C3%A9nie_du_Lac_des_Deux-Montagnes.jpg

3 J.J. O'Neill, CC BY-SA 4.0 <https://creativecommons.org/licenses/by-sa/4.0>, via Wikimedia Commons. https://commons.wikimedia.org/wiki/File:Copper_Inuit_in_an_umiak_at_Port_Epworth_(38553).jpg

4 https://pixabay.com/illustrations/vintage-arthur-rackham-victorian-1722786/

5 Internet Archive Book Images, No restrictions, via Wikimedia Commons. https://commons.wikimedia.org/wiki/File:En_mocassins_(1920)_(14747592616).jpg

6 Lidine Mia, CC BY-SA 4.0 <https://creativecommons.org/licenses/by-sa/4.0>, via Wikimedia Commons: https://commons.wikimedia.org/wiki/File:Plimoth_Plantation_-_Reconstitution_d%27un_campement_d%27am%C3%A9rindiens_Wampanoag._01.jpg

7 https://pixabay.com/illustrations/painting-art-artwork-karl-bodmer-1023411/

8 https://commons.wikimedia.org/wiki/File:Chief_Sitting_Bull.jpg

9 https://commons.wikimedia.org/wiki/File:Battle_of_the_Little_Big_Horn.jpg

10 https://commons.wikimedia.org/wiki/File:Wilma_Mankiller_1998.jpg

11 Tripodero, CC0, via Wikimedia Commons: https://commons.wikimedia.org/wiki/File:Flag_of_the_American_Indian_Movement_V2.svg

12 Mathias Krumbholz, CC BY-SA 3.0 <https://creativecommons.org/licenses/by-sa/3.0>, via Wikimedia Commons: https://commons.wikimedia.org/wiki/File:Stars_01_(MK).jpg

13 https://pixabay.com/illustrations/ai-generated-bear-animal-wild-8666173/

14 Stellarium map with additions by Bob King; source: Robert Benjamin., CC BY-SA 3.0 <https://creativecommons.org/licenses/by-sa/3.0>, via Wikimedia Commons: https://commons.wikimedia.org/wiki/File:Arc-Big-Dipper-map_S2.jpg

15 https://commons.wikimedia.org/wiki/File:Ernest_Smith_Sky_Woman_1936.jpg

16 https://pixabay.com/illustrations/space-stars-comet-astronomy-1486556/

17 https://pixabay.com/illustrations/ai-generated-raven-bird-crow-8525111/

18 https://pixabay.com/illustrations/ai-generated-shaman-mystical-forest-8671770/

19 https://pixabay.com/illustrations/ai-generated-woman-native-american-8549063/

20 Evan Howard, CC BY-SA 2.0 <https://creativecommons.org/licenses/by-sa/2.0>, via Wikimedia Commons: https://commons.wikimedia.org/wiki/File:Bison_Hunt_(24176185315).jpg

21 https://commons.wikimedia.org/wiki/File:Native_Americans_from_Southeastern_Idaho_-_NARA_-_519243.tif

22 https://commons.wikimedia.org/wiki/File:Buffalo_Hunt.jpg

23 Internet Archive Book Images, No restrictions, via Wikimedia Commons: https://commons.wikimedia.org/wiki/File:American_Indians_-_first_families_of_the_Southwest_(1920)_(14589572319).jpg

24 Southwestern State Teachers College, No restrictions, via Wikimedia Commons: https://commons.wikimedia.org/wiki/File:%22Buffalo_in_Western_Okla.%22_(Oklahoma)_Native_American_and_Bison_art_detail,_Oracle,_The_(1921)_(14788226263)_(cropped).jpg

25 https://commons.wikimedia.org/wiki/File:Native_American_Indians.jpg

26 Frithjof Schuon, CC0, via Wikimedia Commons: https://commons.wikimedia.org/wiki/File:Detail_from_%E2%80%9CApparition_of_the_Buffalo_Calf_Maiden%E2%80%9D_(1959)_by_Frithjof_Schuon.jpg

27 Martin St-Amant (S23678), CC BY-SA 3.0 <https://creativecommons.org/licenses/by-sa/3.0>, via Wikimedia Commons: https://commons.wikimedia.org/wiki/File:44_-_Iguazu_-_D%C3%A9cembre_2007.jpg

28 Copetersen www.copetersen.com, CC BY-SA 3.0 <https://creativecommons.org/licenses/by-sa/3.0>, via Wikimedia Commons: https://commons.wikimedia.org/wiki/File:3782_Common_Raven_in_flight.jpg

29 Matthew T Rader, https://matthewtrader.com, CC BY-SA 4.0 <https://creativecommons.org/licenses/by-sa/4.0>, via Wikimedia Commons: https://commons.wikimedia.org/wiki/File:Copper_Breaks_State_Park_with_the_Milky_Way_Galaxy.jpg

30 https://commons.wikimedia.org/wiki/File:Micmac2.jpg

31 Jessie Eastland, CC BY-SA 4.0 <https://creativecommons.org/licenses/by-sa/4.0>, via Wikimedia Commons: https://commons.wikimedia.org/wiki/File:Desert_Electric.jpg

32 California Department of Fish and Wildlife from Sacramento, CA, USA, CC BY 2.0 <https://creativecommons.org/licenses/by/2.0>, via Wikimedia Commons: https://commons.wikimedia.org/wiki/File:Coyote_03_(canis_latrans)_ (22169256854).jpg

33 Tigerhawkvok (talk · contribs), CC BY-SA 3.0 <https://creativecommons.org/licenses/by-sa/3.0>, via Wikimedia Commons: https://commons.wikimedia.org/wiki/File:Crotalus_cerastes_mesquite_springs_ CA.JPG

34 Danielarapava, CC BY-SA 4.0 <https://creativecommons.org/licenses/by-sa/4.0>, via Wikimedia Commons: https://commons.wikimedia.org/wiki/File:Frostedbubble2.jpg

35 Keppler, Udo J., 1872-1956, artist; Poe, Edgar Allan, 1809-1849. Raven., Public domain, via Wikimedia Commons: https://commons.wikimedia.org/wiki/File:%22FREE_SILVER%22_raven_art_in_190 0_detail,_from-_Nevermore_-_Keppler._LCCN2010651343_(cropped).tif

36 https://pixabay.com/illustrations/owl-branch-perch-wise-wisdom-bird-6164884/

37 https://www.pexels.com/photo/photo-of-stream-during-daytime-3225517/

38 Devaprasanna Ghatak, CC BY 4.0 <https://creativecommons.org/licenses/by/4.0>, via Wikimedia Commons: https://commons.wikimedia.org/wiki/File: Spectacularly_colourful_canna_flower_rising_into_a_cloudy_sky.jpg

39 https://pixabay.com/illustrations/mountains-jump-boy-rock-success-7004455/

40 Workman, CC BY-SA 3.0 <https://creativecommons.org/licenses/by-sa/3.0>, via Wikimedia Commons: https://commons.wikimedia.org/wiki/File: Aerial_view_of_canyons.jpg

41 https://pixabay.com/illustrations/native-american-native-american-women-8076731/

42 https://en.wikipedia.org/wiki/File:Detail_Lewis_%26_Clark_at_Three_Forks.jpg

43 https://pixabay.com/illustrations/ai-generated-child-mountain-girl-8672743/

44 See page for author, CC BY 4.0 <https://creativecommons.org/licenses/by/4.0>, via Wikimedia Commons: https://commons.wikimedia.org/wiki/File:A_North _American_Indian_shaman_or_medicine_man_healing_a_pat_Wellcome_V001599 8.jpg

45 https://commons.wikimedia.org/wiki/File:Chief_seattle.jpg

46 Jeffery Hayes, CC BY-SA 3.0 <https://creativecommons.org/licenses/by-sa/3.0>, via Wikimedia Commons: https://commons.wikimedia.org/wiki/File: Seattle_Center_as_night_falls.jpg

47 https://commons.wikimedia.org/wiki/File:Navajo_flag.svg

48 https://commons.wikimedia.org/wiki/File:Navajo_winter_hogan.jpg

49 By Noahedits, CC BY-SA 4.0 <https://creativecommons.org/licenses/by-sa/4.0>, via Wikimedia Commons: https://commons.wikimedia.org/wiki/File:Lakota_map.svg:

50 https://commons.wikimedia.org/wiki/File:En-chief-sitting-bull.jpg

51 https://commons.wikimedia.org/wiki/File:Young-Man-Afraid-of-His-Horses_(Tashun-Kakokipa),_an_Oglala_Sioux,_standing_in_front_of_his_lodge,_Pine_Ridge,_South_Dak_-_NARA_-_530813.jpg

52 By Original Compiled by Aaron Walden.Vector derivative by Jdcollins13, CC BY-SA 3.0 <https://creativecommons.org/licenses/by-sa/3.0>, via Wikimedia Commons: https://commons.wikimedia.org/wiki/File:Great_seal_of_the_cherokee_nation.svg

53 https://commons.wikimedia.org/w/index.php?curid=334447

54 https://commons.wikimedia.org/w/index.php?curid=997266

55 https://commons.wikimedia.org/w/index.php?curid=6735601

56 By Junuxx at Dutch Wikipedia, CC BY-SA 3.0, https://commons.wikimedia.org/w/index.php?curid=1809070

57 Ansgar Walk, CC BY-SA 3.0 <http://creativecommons.org/licenses/by-sa/3.0/>, via Wikimedia Commons https://commons.wikimedia.org/w/index.php?curid=838934

58 Sailko, CC BY 3.0 <https://creativecommons.org/licenses/by/3.0>, via Wikimedia Commons: https://commons.wikimedia.org/wiki/File:Canada,_qaqaq_ashoona,_sedna,_madre_dei_mari,_legno,_1988.JPG

59 https://commons.wikimedia.org/wiki/File:Inupiat_Family_from_Noatak,_Alaska,_1929,_Edward_S._Curtis_(restored).jpg

60 By Ish ishwar (talk · contribs), CC BY-SA 3.0 <http://creativecommons.org/licenses/by-sa/3.0/>, via Wikimedia Commons: https://commons.wikimedia.org/wiki/File:Apachean_present.png:

61 By Kimi Eisele: https://borderlore.org/my-sunrise/: https://borderlore.org/wp-content/gallery/apache-sunrise-ceremony/21-CornPollen.jpg

62 Hopi flag by Mario1952Navajo flag map is my own work, CC BY-SA 4.0 <https://creativecommons.org/licenses/by-sa/4.0>, via Wikimedia Commons https://commons.wikimedia.org/wiki/File:Flag_map_of_the_Hopi_Reservation.png

63 https://commons.wikimedia.org/wiki/File:Hopi_woman_with_a_traditional_pot_and_traditional_clothing.png

64 Cimmyt, Attribution-NonCommercial-ShareAlike 2.0 Generic, BY-NC-SA 2.0 < https://creativecommons.org/licenses/by-nc-sa/2.0/deed.en> https://www.flickr.com/photos/cimmyt/5758809079

65 By Goddard (1996, 1999): https://commons.wikimedia.org/wiki/File:Tlingit-map.png

66 Mharrsch, Attribution-NonCommercial-ShareAlike 2.0 Generic, CC BY-NC-SA 2.0 < https://creativecommons.org/licenses/by-nc-sa/2.0/deed.en> https://www.flickr.com/photos/mharrsch/523470396

67 Pahphotos, Attribution-NonCommercial-NoDerivs 2.0 Generic, CC BY-NC-ND 2.0 <https://creativecommons.org/licenses/by-nc-nd/2.0/deed.en> https://www.flickr.com/photos/pahphotos/3620645429

www.ingramcontent.com/pod-product-compliance
Lightning Source LLC
Chambersburg PA
CBHW061750120626
46550CB00005B/1947